The Church Revealed

by

Dr. Thomas Eristhee

Bloomington, IN 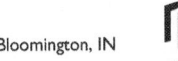 Milton Keynes, UK

authorHOUSE®

AuthorHouse™
1663 Liberty Drive, Suite 200
Bloomington, IN 47403
www.authorhouse.com
Phone: 1-800-839-8640

AuthorHouse™ UK Ltd.
500 Avebury Boulevard
Central Milton Keynes, MK9 2BE
www.authorhouse.co.uk
Phone: 08001974150

First published by AuthorHouse 10/27/2006

ISBN: 1-4259-5378-6 (sc)

Library of Congress Control Number: 2006906781

Printed in the United States of America
Bloomington, Indiana

This book is printed on acid-free paper.

Table Of Contents

Introduction

It is very important to have the right understanding of the New Testament doctrine of the church, since it is the pattern we should follow. Also, there are lots of misconceptions about what constitutes the church and how it should function: what organization is the right church, and whether there is a need for Pastors, Bishops and Elders in the church. In addition, in some modern day churches, there is a great departure from the New Testament doctrine of the church.

It seems to me that some people are afraid of where the church will eventually end up. We hear of so much corruption, immorality, and all kinds of allegations against the leadership and members of the present day church, as well as local congregations and independent groups. So, there is fear among many sincere individuals concerning the future of the church. But when we read the New Testament, we have a very clear understanding of the final destination of the church of Jesus Christ.

In order for us to enjoy all the blessings of God, we must be part of His church. Therefore, we need to understand the doctrine of the church so that we can be a part of it and enjoy the benefits thereof, and usher in those who are not yet part of the church so that they might be recipients of the blessings that are to be enjoyed by members of the church.

I do not want to over emphasize the importance of such a study, but Jesus Christ came to build His church. He loves the church; He died for the church, He is protecting and watching over the church, and He will come again for His church. We are very important people since Jesus Christ purchased the church with His precious blood.

The Scripture calls the church "Beloved of God", "Partakers of His Divine Nature", "Children of God", "Joint heirs with Christ", "Elect according to the foreknowledge of God", "Sanctified", "Glorified". As partakers of like precious faith as the apostles; members are referred to as; "Saints, being washed in the blood of Jesus, sanctified, justified in the name of the Lord Jesus Christ and by the Spirit of God". They are described as being born again, being raised from the dead, being quickened by the Holy Spirit; and Jesus went to prepare a special place for them.

My desire is that this book will give the believer a greater understanding of the church which he is part of, and that the believer may have a biblical understanding of the church which will create an unquenchable thirst in his heart to be part of this beautiful structure that God has put together.

May the Lord of the Church bless you.

The Church Defined

The church is everywhere, yet many people don't have a clue as to what the church is. There are people who are part of the church, but don't understand the church. The Bible says that Abraham is the father of the faithful believers; because it was by faith that Abraham became a child of God, and this is how the true believers become children of God – through faith in Jesus Christ. In the Old Testament, God had a people – He had a covenant with them. These people were under a covenant with Him; but when the New Testament came, He made a new covenant with all those who would accept Jesus as their Lord and Savior.

Now, He is not dealing with the children of Israel only; but in this new covenant – He is dealing with all the nations of the world. It is for "whosoever will". As *John 3:16* says, *"For God so loved the world, that He gave His Only Begotten Son, that whosoever believeth in Him shall not perish but have everlasting life"*. So He died for everybody; and whosoever believes in Him will receive everlasting life. The church is

1

not Israel; and when you become a child of God you do not become a Jew, but you become a member of the church of Jesus Christ.

For those who believe they become a Jew after their conversion; hear what the apostle to the gentiles says in *1 Corinthians 10: 32*, *"Give none offence, neither to the Jews, nor to the gentiles, nor to the church of God"*. So, we see here from this portion of scripture, that there are three different entities on earth; three different groups of people - Jews, Gentiles and the Church of Jesus Christ. So we belong to one of these groups according to the words of the Holy Bible.

A long time ago, religious people who did not understand the true church of Jesus Christ had been trying to marry the church with other things or groups - but the church stands by itself. You cannot mix the church with any other group - this is a new thing. Hear what Jesus had to say when the Scribes and Pharisees saw Him eating with publicans and sinners, not holding the traditions of the Jewish church in *Mark 2: 21 - 22*.

Jesus says, *"No man also seweth a piece of new cloth on an old garment: else the new piece that filled it up taketh away from the old, and the rent is made worse. And no man putteth new wine into old bottles: else the new wine doth burst the bottles, and the wine is spilled, and the bottles will be marred; but new wine must be put into new bottles"*.

Christianity cannot be mixed with Judaism. The new life the believer finds in Jesus cannot be mixed with the Jews' religion. They are two different things - two different covenants; and

2

the new is better than the old. If you mix them you will lose both the bottle and the wine – they just cannot be mixed. In the book of Acts, when the Spirit of God fell, it did not fall on the religious Jewish people who were not converted; it fell on the hundred and twenty that were in the upper room, who had trusted in Jesus Christ as their Lord and Savior. Who had repented of their sins and were baptized as Jesus had commanded.

Now let us remember there were a lot of people in Jerusalem on that day, including religious people and devoted Jews; but they never accepted Jesus as their Lord and Savior. So they were there in their rituals and forms, while the followers of Jesus were waiting for the promise of the Holy Spirit; and they received Him – the Holy Spirit was poured upon them.

Then this was noised abroad. People who came from every nation were present in Jerusalem for the religious festival, filled with religion without God. When they heard of what was happening where the true church was gathered, they came. Some mocked, some said the disciples were mad; but Peter stood and preached unto them. Some believed; (about three thousand). They asked him, "What must we do?" He said unto them, "Repent and be baptized". Now some of these people were strong in the Jewish religion, but when they believed in Jesus Christ, they abandoned their Jewish traditions and were baptized, and continued in the apostles' doctrine and fellowship and breaking of bread. They did not go back to their old dead religion – they were part of the true church.

Dr. Thomas Eristhee

The word "Church"

The word "church" is never referred to as an Organization. It is a group of people; it is at times referred to as a local congregation – all believers in a locality; for example, the church at Ephesus. The church is the people who have submitted themselves to the rule of God over their lives; and are governed by His Word. Just as Israel was called out of Egypt, so the church is called out of the world; out of the rule of the devil, to serve God in spirit and in truth. The church is God's flock (His sheep), and He is their Shepherd. Members of the church are brothers because they are all bought with the same blood – the blood of Jesus Christ. They are all sons and daughters of God, through redemption; they have been restored through the work of Jesus Christ on the cross. He paid the price of their redemption.

Church & State

The church is mentioned in the news media, but no one defines the church. So many, many listeners are lost as to the message that is being sent out. Some say the church is to be separated from the state. If the church is separated from the state, what type of state will we have? Jesus says that the church is the light of the world and the salt of the earth. Can you imagine a country without light and salt? It would be chaos.

Let us hear what Solomon had to say about the matter; bearing in mind that he was a king and the wisest man who ever lived. *Proverbs 29: 2* says, *"When the righteous are in authority, the people rejoice: but when the wicked beareth rule, the people mourn"*. Because of the ignorance of the church on these matters, we have stayed out of politics with have allowed wicked men with no good character to lead our nations. Many of them have no fear of God, but are very respectful to the ideas of Satan. Therefore, these men, when they are in authority, legislate laws that are contrary to the Word of God, and therefore contrary to the church. When these things happen, the church wants to pray.

5

Now, I strongly believe in the power of prayer, but God will not go against His Word. The Word says when the wicked rule the people mourn; so what the church has to do is to deal with the root of the problem – put righteous people in Authority, and you will have righteous rule. You cannot put an alcoholic to guard a Rum Shop – the temptation will be too great.

I would like to remind us that the Jews were saved from Haman's plot not because they fasted and prayed, but because they also used their influence – Esther's position in the Government. She was the king's wife and therefore used her position to talk to the king and made the king change his mind from passing a law that Haman, an enemy of God's people, wanted to pass which would have killed all of God's people in that particular Providence. But Esther used her position and influence to change things around.

The church must pray but the church must also rise and take its position on earth. God has given to members of His church talents to govern, administrate and to rule; but like in the parable of the talents, we are hiding our talents and our excuse is that we are afraid. We do not know that we can use our gift in a governmental position to do something for the poor, something for the homeless; and to bring changes in the legal system. Let us look again at the Divinely Inspired Word of God on the matter.

In the New Testament – **Romans 13: 1-5**, *"Let every soul be subject unto the higher powers. For there is no power but of God: the powers that be are ordained of God. Whosoever therefore resisteth the power, resisteth the ordinance of God: and they that resist shall receive to themselves damnation.*

For rulers are not a terror to good works, but to the evil. Will thou then not be afraid of the power? Do that which is good, and thou shall have praise of the same. For he is the minister of God to thee for good. But if thou do that which is evil, be afraid; for he beareth not the sword in vain. For he is the minister of God, a revenger to execute wrath upon him that doeth evil. Wherefore ye must needs be subject, not only for wrath, but also for conscience sake".

Here this portion of Scripture is telling us that we must be subject to the higher powers. How can you as a Christian be in subjection to a government that is contrary to the word of God? Supposing this government says that you must not mention the name of Jesus in your prayers or in your church, will you obey him? Of course not!

In such a case the principle of the apostles in **Acts 4:17 - 20** will stand which reads, *"But that it spread no further among the people, let us straightly threaten them that they speak henceforth to no man in that name. And they called them, and commanded them not to speak at all nor teach in the name of Jesus. But Peter and John answered and said unto them, whether it be right in the sight of God to hearken unto you more than unto God, judge ye".*

The point I am trying to make is that the Word of God teaches us to obey authority, because it is God's design that we have leadership in the country; however, the leaders must be righteous, and so we who are involved in the process of electing them should elect righteous people, and should encourage people of integrity who have the leadership abilities to be in government. When we have godly people in authority, we will have a prosperous country. Because the Bible says in **Proverbs 14: 34 - 35**, *"Righteousness exalteth a nation, but sin is a reproach to any people. The king's favor is towards a wise servant: but his wrath is against him that causeth shame".*

Making Disciples - The Work Of Ministry

The church is not sent out in its own power for Jesus says, "...after that the Holy Ghost comes upon you, you shall receive power." When we go out to make disciples, we recognize that we cannot do it without power. The devil has the people bound, blind and dead; so we need a greater power working in us to be able to set the people free. God has given us the Holy Spirit to effectively communicate the gospel to the lost.

To make disciples, we have been given the means to be effective. You may say, "what is the means" or "how can I be effective?" Let us read it from the Bible – *Acts 1:8*, *"But ye shall receive power after that the Holy Ghost is come upon you: and ye shall be witnesses unto me both in Jerusalem, and in all Judea, and in Samaria, and unto the uttermost parts of the earth"*. To be effective you need power – Holy Ghost power. God promised to give us that power. Therefore, we must ask Him to give it to us. That power is to make us effective witnesses everywhere we go.

Now, the disciples bore witness of Christ before they were filled with the Holy Spirit. For we read in the Bible before the outpouring of the Holy Spirit in Acts and before the death and resurrection of Jesus Christ in **Luke 10: 17**, *"And the seventy returned again with joy saying, Lord, even the devils are subject unto us through thy name"*. So they were doing the work of God and casting out demons, but they did not have the kind of success that they got after they were filled with the Holy Spirit. By the way, Jesus Himself did the work of the kingdom, and bore witness to the fact that God was his Father by the anointing of the Holy Spirit upon Him.

Jesus said it many times in the Bible. In **Luke 4: 18 - 19** He said, *"The spirit of the Lord is upon me, because he hath anointed me to preach the gospel to the poor; he hath sent me to heal the brokenhearted, to preach deliverance to the captives, and recovering of sight to the blind; to set at liberty them that are bruised, to preach the acceptable year of the Lord"*.

So, it was the Holy Spirit who gave Him the enablement to do it. Again in **Matthew 12:28**, He makes it clear that He casts out devils by the Spirit of God. Now, more than ever before the church is greatly challenged to perform that aspect of ministry because of the multitudes that are possessed with devils. And, nobody can deliver those who are possessed but those who have the anointing of the Holy Spirit upon their lives, because Satan will not cast out Satan. Thank God, the power of the Holy Spirit was not just available for Jesus and the disciples only, but it is available for the church today.

If we are to reach our people, we had better have supernatural power flowing from us, because there is evil power in their lives. But we can reach the world by the ability that the Holy Spirit gives. If the eyes of the blind are being opened, if the possessed are being delivered, the lame are walking, dead are being raised, people will not be able to deny that God is working with us. Jesus said to the unbelievers of His day - if you would not believe me for what I say, believe me for the work that I do.

The church must not try to do the work of God without the Spirit of God. This will lead to frustration and burn-outs. We must depend on the Holy Spirit totally, because by ourselves we are nothing. When the lame man who was crippled from his mother's womb got healed, the people knew that this was the work of God. This was bearing witness that Jesus was alive and working in the church and meeting the needs of the people. They could not deny the miracle for everyone in the area knew the man who was made whole.

True & False Churches

How can one become a member of the Church?

There are people and groups, who claim to be the church or part of the church, and are not. Just as you have people saying they are Jews and are not; people say they belong to the church of Christ and they do not. There are some people who genuinely think that they are part of the church, and are not; and there are people who are in the congregation who know that they are not part of the church. Some of them have been sent by Satan on special assignments, to try to hinder the progress of the church and at times to bring confusion in the church, to oppose the leadership, to promote immorality and to try to hinder prayers.

We read again in *Revelation 2: 9*, "*I know thy works, and tribulation, and poverty, (but thou art rich) and I know the blasphemy of them which say they are Jews and are not, but are of the synagogue of Satan*". We see that there was a group of people among the church who were not part of the church. As a matter of fact, God says that they were from the church of Satan. Yet, they came in the midst of the people of God, and believe you me, Satan has not changed this strategy of sending his messengers among the people of God.

In *Revelation 2:20*, God is talking to His church about what He does not like. Here is what He says. *"Notwithstanding I have a few things against thee, because thou sufferest that woman Jezebel, which calleth herself a prophetess, to teach and to seduce my servants to commit fornication and to eat things sacrificed unto idols"*. Here, we see a woman in the church who deceived the leadership into believing that she was true and was a messenger of God; but she was not, and her fruits were evil. But the church did not recognize that she was false until God revealed it to them.

The apostle Paul before his encounter with God on the road to Damascus thought he was saved. He thought he was a child of God, a member of the church; yet he was killing those who said they were God's children because he thought that these people were not following the right tradition. But when he had the encounter with God he realized that he was wrong and that those he was trying to kill were right. So after his conversion, he became part of them. The first step to being part of the church of Jesus Christ is - you must have an encounter with God. You must ask Him to forgive your sins, and you must recognize that Jesus is the only Savior of the world. He died for our sins and rose from the dead after three days, and He ascended into Heaven – He is Lord of all! Without accepting Christ as your only Savior, you cannot be a part of His church.

Jesus said to Nicodemus, a religious man: "You must be born again." That can only happen by asking Jesus to come into your life and making you a new man, forgiving you of all your sins and making you His child. This is important because we have all gone astray from God. We are all unworthy and there is nothing we can do to make us worthy except having our sins forgiven. The only way we can have our sins forgiven is based on what Christ has done for us. He died in our place, and so we must accept that fact: that God can accept us. We cannot put new life in ourselves. It is God who is the author of life – we must ask Him to put new spiritual life in us. It is Christ who gives us power to become the sons of God. Not of works of righteousness that we do, it is the gift of God. All you need to do is to ask Him. In the process of becoming a child of God, (i.e. being born again, a member of the church) God gives us a clean heart, a new spirit. He makes us a new man; and that happens immediately after we ask Him to do it – once we are serious.

The process is mysterious. It is spiritual – it is a work of God. In *John 3:8* Jesus compares it to the wind that blows and we cannot tell where it comes from and where it is going. It reads, *"The wind bloweth where it listeth, and thou hearest the sound thereof, but canst not tell whence it cometh, and wither it goeth. So is every one that is born of the Spirit"*. When God has done His work in us of giving us new life, others will see the effect of the work in our lives – they will see the change. It can be compared to a strong wind passing through a banana field. You may not have been there when it passed, but you will see the effect of the wind in that field.

Once one is a member of the church, he cannot continue living in sin because of the change that has taken place in his life. Now I do not mean he cannot commit an act of sin – he will make mistakes – but he will not willfully practice sin. Sinning for him is "if" and not "when". The Scripture says in *1John 3:8*, *"He that commit sin is of the devil; for the devil sinned from the beginning. For this purpose the Son of God was manifested, that He might destroy the works of the devil"*. So the new life in Christ, gives us victory over our sin and the devil.

The true people of God live holy lives. Those who say they are children of God, part of the church, and are still living in sin have not been born from above. Remember it is by their fruits you shall know them. A good tree cannot bring forth evil fruit, and an evil tree cannot bring forth good fruit. You cannot be of God and your fruits are evil. The true church holds to the Word of God as its final authority. No man or counsel or committee is above the Word of God. The Word of God is the final authority whether the church likes it or not. They must accept it, believe it, and teach what the Bible says and not their views, feelings or opinion. If the Word of God is not being adhered to by the people who claim to be the church, then they are false. This is what we read in *John 8: 31 - 32*, *"Then said Jesus to those Jews which believed on him; If ye continue in my words, then are ye my disciples indeed; and ye shall know the truth, and the truth shall make you free"*.

No one who preaches another gospel than that which is recorded in the sixty-six books of the Holy Scriptures belongs to the Lord. No one who removes or adds to it belongs to the

Lord. The duty of the church is to obey the Word of God. Paul says we should not allow any man to prevent us from obeying the true gospel of Christ. This is what we read in *Galatians 1: 6 - 8*, "*I marvel that ye are so soon removed from him that called you into the grace of Christ unto another gospel. Which is not another, but there be some that trouble you, and would pervert the gospel of Christ; But though we, or an angel from heaven, preach any other gospel unto you than that which we have preached unto you, let him be accursed*".

I would now like to draw your attention to one more portion of Scripture on this matter, because it is a very serious matter and Scripture is being fulfilled right before our very eyes. *Revelation 20* says, "*And if any man shall take away from the words of the book of this prophecy, God shall take away his part out of the book of life, and out of the holy city, and from the things which are written in this book*".

To me, these are serious warnings to those who believe in tampering with the Word of God. It seems to me that there are lots of people nowadays who think that they know right and wrong better than God Himself. So, what I have observed is that if there is something in the Bible that they cannot comprehend or don't agree with, they take it out. For example, the Bible is clear about a burning Hell to those who reject Christ and die in a sinful condition. We are told where their final destination will be; but, because some people have their own subjective interpretation about a loving God, they say a loving God will not send any body to hell, and therefore no matter how clear God's Word is on the matter, they ignore it and try to change it.

Yes! There are some who will even re-write the Bible to remove certain verses or phrases that they don't like from the original Word of God. I say to you such people do not belong to the true church of God; they have been deceived by the serpent along with their followers. Allow me to give another example because I spoke about those who take away from the Word of God - those who add to the Word of God. There is no difference in the punishment - they are both evil.

There are many religions and people who will not deny the Word of God, they would not deny that there is a Hell and a Heaven; but they don't agree with the fact that there is only one way to enter heaven - and this is through Jesus Christ alone. As He stated in *John 14:6*, *"Jesus saith unto him, I am the way the truth and the life; no man cometh unto the Father, but by me"*. But some are trying to enter through Mohammed through what the Koran says. Others are trying to enter based on their good works as if to say they can pay their way to Heaven - they have worked for that. Yet, there are those who teach we can get there through the Sacraments, through the Rosary - that our loved ones can pay some religious leader to say prayers for us, that we might be accepted into Heaven after we have passed away.

Yes, they have added about fifteen more books to the Bible and have placed them as equal to the infallible, un-adulterated Word of God. They call them the Apocrypha. Many of the things that are written in these books are contrary to the Word of God. But, in some "churches" they read it as if it were the Word of God. As a matter of fact, after it is read to the congregation, the minister says many times, "this is the word of the Lord". And the blind flock that just don't know any better, will answer sincerely but sadly wrong – "thanks be to God". What will I say to these people who go to such "churches"? Come out from among them and repent. Ask Jesus to save you and find a church that preaches the Word of God without compromising it. Friends, the true church will not pray to any dead saint. No! Not even to Mary – the mother of Jesus Christ. Neither will the true church bow to idols.

Hear what the Word says on this matter. In *1 Timothy2: 5*, *"For there is one God, and one mediator between God and man, the man Christ Jesus"*. Not two – one; and this is Jesus Christ. He is the ONLY Mediator for both man and woman. Nobody understands you like Jesus. Mary did not die for us; Jesus did. He is the one who sits at the right hand of the Father making intercessions for us. Now, some would say, "Preacher, what about all these people from all these nations who are so devoted and sincere in worshipping idols and have had angels appearing to them, and miracles happening among them"? They have some great preachers who show such great concern for the people that they are powerful – What saith thou? Let us go to the Bible for the answer. *2 Corinthians11: 13 - 14* states, *"For such are false apostles, deceitful workers, transforming themselves into the apostles of Christ. And no marvel; for Satan himself is transformed into an angel of light"*.

My dearly beloved, the devil is cunning. He will come as a minister of God, as a good angel, just to keep you in darkness. He will anoint his preachers to do his work; he may even use them from time to time to perform miracles. Let us be reminded that he can perform some miracles and if he has to perform miracles to keep people in bondage – he will do it. It will look so real that you would not be able to discern that it was done by the devil. After all, he is the devil, the old serpent who deceived the whole world. Therefore, I say unto you, know the Word of God because it is the sword of the Spirit. Jesus in **Matthew Chapter 4** used the word against Satan. We must not do anything that is against the Word of God; for everything that seeks to influence us to do things contrary to the Word of God – is false.

The apostle John in concluding his first epistle wrote to the church and said in **1 John 5:21,** "Little children, keep yourselves from idols. Amen". In **1 Corinthians 12:2** the apostle Paul says, *"Ye know that ye were gentiles, carried away unto these dumb idols, even as ye were led"*. Before we were saved, we were involved in this "stuff" he called it "dumb idols". In other words, it cannot do anything for you. It is just a piece of art, and how then are you bowing to it and making sacrifices to it? In the true sense of the word, Paul is saying this is spiritual madness; and the church of Jesus Christ should not engage in such practices.

Let us again hear Paul in **2 Corinthians 6: 16 - 17,** *"And what agreement hath the temple of God with idols? For ye are the temple of the living God; as God hath said, I will dwell in them, and walk in them, and I will be their God and they shall be my people. Wherefore, come out from among them, and be ye separate saith the Lord; and touch not the unclean thing, and I will receive you"*. From these Scriptures, it is absolutely clear that the church of Jesus Christ has nothing to do with idols; and I can give many Scriptures that speak against idol worship. My intention is to prove from the Scriptures that the true members of Christ's church are not involved in any form of idol worship. We enter the true church through Jesus Christ alone by asking Him to save us. We must believe in His finished work on the cross for us. We must acknowledge that we are lost without Him, and in Him we are complete!

Church Discipline

Right through the Old Testament, we saw God disciplining His people; and there are countless passages that talk about discipline. Not to have discipline in the church is to have chaos. A house without discipline will bring shame to the leaders of the house. If God's church does not have discipline, then it is not God's church. In **Titus 1:5** Paul says, *"For this cause left I thee in Crete, that thou shouldest set in order the things that are wanting, and ordain elders in every city as I have appointed thee"*. So Paul is saying here that Titus, who was the Pastor of that church, had to put things in order in that particular church; and to put leadership in place in the other churches.

In **Numbers 16**, we see one of the worse forms of punishment in the entire Bible where Korah and his group rebelled against Moses and Aaron. When Moses asked them to come and talk about the matter, they stated twice in the chapter, *"we will not come up"* - now this is rebellion. Let us read the punishment that the Lord gave them in **Numbers16: 31 - 35**. *"And it came* *to pass, as he had made an end of speaking all these words, that the ground clave asunder that was under them; and the earth opened her mouth and swallowed them up, and their houses, and all the men that appertained unto Korah, and all their goods. They, and all that appertained to them, went down alive into the pit, and the earth closed upon them: and they perished from among the congregation; and all Israel that were round about them, fled at the cry of them. For they said, lest the earth swallow us up also; and there came out a fire from the Lord, and consumed the two hundred and fifty men that offered incense".*

God is not interested in killing His children, but when we refuse to obey after all effort has been exhausted, strong measures must be taken that others may fear. We see in the Scriptures, Ananias and his wife Sapphira lying to the apostle Peter about their giving, and God "took them out" that very moment. What am I saying? I am saying that God is very serious about discipline in His church. He wants His church to resemble Him and He scarcely takes extreme measures because His purpose is to save and to restore. But, there are times that He does take extreme measures. In addition, His leaders take extreme measures based on the sin and the attitude of the offending brother.

However, what I have observed happening nowadays among the Body of Christ in the context of discipline, is that due to our lack of principle, when a church disciplines a brother, he walks out instead of staying in that church and admitting that he has faltered. He should take time to be restored, learn from the discipline that was given to him and follow the directives of the congregation. But instead, he goes to another congregation and right away, that pastor who has no discipline or does things for other reasons, receives this brother who has been placed on discipline by his former pastor. But the brother has never taken the disciplinary measures that he was placed under. As a matter of fact, that is why he left the congregation he was in.

You may say, "Bishop, what is wrong with that?" Well, it seems to me that this person is living under rebellion - he left the first church bound - so he enters the second bound. Did we not read in *Matthew18: 17*, that, if he does not hear the church he is *"as an heathen man and a publican"*. He must make it right with the first church before he can be free. God gave the church power to bind and to loose in this instance. The church must deal with sin. We cannot harbor sin in our midst, and those who cover sin will not prosper. Parents discipline their children when they do things that are wrong. The Bible says God disciplines His children and the pastor who is over the church of the living God must discipline those whom God has put in his care.

The disciplinary action must cause the person to recognize his mistake and turn from his evil ways. For example, disfellowship, (that is he is no more in fellowship with his brothers and sisters), should cause him to correct his wrong doing, so that he might be restored to his rightful position in the church. We cannot be living in sin and be puffed up about it. Godly sorrow leads to repentance - not rebellion and pride. In my opinion, one should not be excommunicated if this is the first time he or she commits that sin, and is sorry about it. But if it is a habit that he/she refuses to correct, then one must take action. Remember, brethren, the church is the temple of God – the ground and pillar of truth, the light of the world. Therefore, we must try to keep it pure.

Let us look at some more Scriptures. In *2Thessalonians 3:6* we read, "*Now we command you brethren, in the name of our Lord Jesus Christ, that ye withdraw yourselves from every brother that walketh disorderly, and not after the tradition which he received of us*". Paul gave a command to the brethren that they withdraw themselves from every brother that walketh disorderly who does not live as the Bible has ordered him to walk. Before we proceed, let us look at another Scripture.

1Corinthians 5:9 - 13 says, "*I wrote unto you in an epistle not to company with fornicators; yet not altogether with the fornicators of the world, or with idolaters; for then must ye needs go out of the world. But now I have written unto you not to keep company. If any man that is called a brother be a fornicator, or covetous, or an extortioner; with such an one do not eat. For what have I to do to judge them also that are without? Do not ye judge them that are within? But them that are without God judgeth. Therefore, put away from among yourselves that wicked person*".

He is saying that he had written them a letter before, telling them what to do with those in the church who walk contrary to the teachings of the Bible. In the first letter he said not to keep company with such persons. He made it clear that he was not talking about the non-Christians but people in the church. So now he is writing again and he is making himself abundantly clear, that he is talking about those who call themselves "children of God"- members of the church, who live as children of the world. He says, "If any man that is called a brother be a fornicator, or covetous or an idolater, or a railer or a drunkard, or an extortioner, with such an one - no not to eat.

This does not mean that we are just to withdraw ourselves from this person and he/she is still in our midst doing as he/she pleases – No, we must make a statement to the local church, letting them know that this person is not in fellowship with the body. He has been disciplined because of his conduct. The leadership doesn't necessarily have to go in details with the congregation, but should let them know the offending brother was disciplined in accordance with the Scripture. Unfortunately, there are people who have gone very far, and all efforts to restore them have failed. We have to separate ourselves from such persons.

Paul says, *"But them that are without God judgeth. Therefore, put away from among yourselves that wicked person"*. It cannot be clearer than that. If there are people in the church who are involved in such sins as are recorded in this portion of Scripture and else where in the Bible, the leadership must take action against such persons. Talk to that individual and try your best to get him back on the right track. We are there to save lives, but let us remember if we don't take action against the offending brother/sister, we would soon find a cancer that will spread in the entire body and destroy the church; and when we want to operate, it might be too late – it may have already spread too far. As Paul says in *1 Corinthians 5: 6 - 7*, *"Your glorying is not good. Know ye not that a little leaven leaveneth the whole lump? Purge out therefore the old leaven, that ye*

27

may be a new lump, as ye are unleavened. For even Christ our Passover is sacrificed for us".

I know it is hard to discipline people in the church. It breaks your heart as a pastor to know that you have to take such drastic action at times; even to excommunicate. This is not easy, but we have to do it because the Bible has instructed us about how to handle certain problems in the church. And we cannot pretend that we have more compassion than Christ or the apostles. The church is not a place for people to live in immorality. And if we don't discipline that immoral person, he will eventually corrupt the whole church. Many times, the leaders who do not discipline their members have "skeletons" in their closets; so it is "I watch your back – you watch mine".

The members of the true church of Jesus Christ stand for righteousness and seek to live righteous lives. Now I say again, that this does not mean that a child of God will not make a mistake; but a mistake is a mistake and not a habit. A habit is not a mistake. It is a lifestyle. Could you imagine the one who drives your vehicle to take your son or daughter to school being involved in an accident every single day because he is making the same mistake every time he reaches a certain bend? Would you allow him to continue driving your bus or continue taking your children to school? Of course not! You would take your keys from him, or send him back to the driving school. If he refuses, you will fire him because he is not just a danger to himself, but to others also.

Any church where people do as they please and are not disciplined is a perfect environment for demons and the ideal repellant to the Holy Spirit.

When The Leader Sins

The pastor must try to maintain the purity of the church.

How do you discipline a pastor who has gone astray? Well, I don't think it is something for the congregation to do; but a Counsel of Elders. The accusation must be by at least two persons according to **1Timothy5:19**, *"Against an elder receive not an accusation, but before two or three witnesses"*. I believe the reason why the Scripture says so is to protect the leader; because a person can fabricate lies simply because they don't like the leader. But the passage went on to say in **verse 20**, *"Them that sin rebuke before all, that others also may fear"*. The Counsel of Elders that would carry out the discipline of an elder should not cover up for that elder who has sinned. The Bible says he must be rebuked before all that others may fear. No one who is a servant of sin should lead the church of Jesus Christ.

The pastor or elder must be blameless. The moral qualifications for being the leader of the church of Jesus Christ are very high.

The purpose is not to deter men from the office because the Scriptures says it is "a good work", and God is able to keep us from falling. Who He calls, He also anoints to do the job. He never calls a servant and doesn't give him what it takes to be able to function where He calls him. Therefore, we should not fear. No one should be the leader of the church of the living God just because he is brilliant, gifted and willing. He must have the moral qualifications also – and the Bible gives a whole list of them. No Counsel or Church should lower the standard that God has set up. What the Scripture says must be followed and we must not be partial in the church of the living God.

The place of leadership in the church of Jesus Christ is not to fill a vacancy. This is a spiritual calling and position and God is the one who decides the requirements. To lead God's church you must be in agreement with God. His church is His Body on earth and as leaders of His church here, we assume the physical headship here on earth. Therefore, the head must be clean, because if the head is sick – the whole body is sick. You see the church is God's house, God's people - His family. Therefore, the leader of this house must be above reproach. It is sad, but it seems that leaders in the churches nowadays could commit any sin they wish; and when they are caught just say sorry, and in a few months they are back in that same leadership position that they were in before.

It seems to me, from the Scriptures, that there are some sins that disqualify a leader from the position of leadership, although he may receive forgiveness from God and the congregation. You see, when a leader sins, his sin becomes the sin of the people he leads. For example, if a member of the congregation commits fornication it affects the church; but it is worse when it is the pastor who does it. When the pastor does it, the media publicizes it. Why? Because he is the leader. The Bible says that although God forgave King David after he had committed adultery with Bathsheba, there were great consequences for his sins.

Let us hear what the Bible says in *2 Samuel 12:10 - 14*, *"Now therefore the sword shall never depart from thine house; because thou hast despised me, and hast taken the wife of Uriah the Hittite to be thy wife. Thus saith the Lord, behold I will raise up evil against thee out thine own house; and I will take thy wives before thine eyes, and give them unto thy neighbor and he shall lie with thy wives in the sight of this sun. For thou didst it secretly: but I will do this thing before all Israel, and before the sun. And David said unto Nathan, I have sinned against the Lord. And Nathan said unto David, the Lord also hath put away thy sin; thou shall not die. Howbeit, because by this deed thou hast given great occasion to the enemies of the Lord to blaspheme, the child also that is born unto thee shall surely die"*.

God said that He had forgiven him; yet there were great consequences - great punishment for his actions. God allowed men to sleep with his wives openly and the child died, even though David fasted to prevent this from happening. There was also division in his house, and incest in his family and we can go on and on. The Bible says it was because he had done these immoral deeds and had given the enemies of the Lord occasion to blaspheme. When we sin as leaders, there are great consequences. And there are some sins we should never commit as leaders of the church of the living God, because we are giving the enemy cause to blaspheme. We are shaming our families and the church of God, the Organization or Group which we represent, the community, nation and of course, the Body of Christ worldwide.

Church Membership

How does one become a member of the local church? Is that so important since once you are saved, you are a member of the church of Jesus Christ? Well, let us see what the Scriptures say since it is our final Authority and not our conscience, opinion or feelings. In the book of **Hebrews 10: 23-25** we read, "*Let us hold fast the profession of our faith without wavering* (for He is faithful that promised), *and let us consider one another to provoke unto love and to good works. Not forsaking the assembling of yourselves together, as the manner of some is; but exhorting one another; and so much the more, as ye see the day approaching*". This portion of Scripture is asking those who are saved to assemble together. It is also saying that there were some, at the time the apostles were writing, who were forsaking the coming together of the believers. So, he warns us not to be like those who forsake the gathering together of the saints.

Some will say this portion of Scripture does not teach church membership, because you can attend church and not be a member of the church. We will get into that in a while. But do you know why some people don't want to be a member of any church? It is because they don't want to be held responsible or accountable. They are not interested in working for the Lord because if they were members, they would have to give a report or an account of their actions or be involved in the church. But when they are not members, they can come and sit in church on Sunday mornings, return to their homes, live in fornication or adultery or any other sin; and nobody can tell them any thing because they are not members.

But, my friends, God wants accountability in His church. The pastor must give an account, and the members likewise. Without accountability, there is no assurance that what is required will be done. Can you imagine going to the Bank to give the teller your money? He does not give you a receipt, neither does he lodge the money into your account and you don't know the teller's name or his address. It was Terry Wise who said, "People do what we inspect and not what we expect". All through the Bible we see the principle of accountability. From Genesis, Adam had to give God an account of his actions. The leaders Moses put over the people had to give an account of the people that were in their care. The spies, when they came back, had to give a report of the trip they were sent on. The disciples had to give an account to Jesus after Jesus sent them on a particular mission. Paul and Barnabas came back to their home church and gave an account of their mission.

There are many stories of accountability of both members and leaders in the Bible that we can look at. But, nowadays, people are looking for excuses for not being members of a local church. As I said before, one of the reasons is they don't want to be accountable.

Remember, without accountability no one gets blamed, no one gets caught, no one gets corrected, no one gets punished. In the book of *Acts 2: 41 - 42* we read, *"Then they that gladly received his word were baptized: and the same day there were added unto them about three thousand souls. And they continued steadfastly in the apostles' doctrine and fellowship, and in breaking of bread, and in prayers"*. Here we see that after Peter preached, those who truly believed were baptized. The Scripture says about three thousand, which seems to indicate that they knew their members. But it went further to say that they were baptized and that they continued steadfastly in the apostles' doctrine, fellowship, breaking of bread and in prayers. So whatever the apostles taught, that was what they accepted as their teaching. Now, the teachings of the apostles were not contrary to Jesus' teachings.

They taught church discipline and they taught accountability of members to the church. The people were also taught to use their talents in the Body of Christ. We read from the Word that they continued in fellowship. They were in communion with each other. They were in prayers with each other and, if we read *verse 46* it says, *"And they continuing daily with one accord in the temple and breaking bread from house to house, did eat their meat with gladness and singleness of heart"*. So, they were in church together, and they knew one another's houses since they had communion together - they were members of a local body.

Let us look at the story where Peter and John were used by God to heal the man who was crippled from his mother's womb, and was about forty years old. The rulers of the day arrested them because they realized that although Jesus was not there physically, great miracles were being done through the disciples and they commanded Peter and John not to speak in the name of Jesus Christ again. Of course, they did not obey the rulers on that matter because they made it very clear to the leaders that Jesus is alive, and that it was in His name that the miracles were taking place.

There is power in the name of Jesus. But what I want you to observe is that after the rulers released them, the Scriptures says in *Acts 4:23*, *"And being let go, they went to their own company and reported all that the chief priests and elders had said unto them"*. The point is that these disciples had a church that they associated with and where they went and reported what they had done and what had happened to them. The beloved Apostle John writing concerning the church and the behavior of some of the members of that particular church - now there were some he commended for their good behavior and there was at least one whom he was very disappointed with for his behavior. Let us look at the member that he was disappointed with in *3 John 9 - 10* which reads, *"I wrote unto the church: but Diotrephes, who loveth to have the pre-eminence among them; recieveth us not. Wherefore, if I come, I will remember his deeds which he doeth, prating against us with malicious words: and not content therewith, neither doth he himself receive the brethren; and forbiddeth them that would, and casteth them out of the church"*.

Here, we have a particular brother in the church who wanted to have the preeminence. John knew him by name, and the members of the church told the apostles about his actions. It seems John would send certain leaders in that particular church to preach or to minister otherwise. But Diotrephes would not allow him, and the members who would reserve the persons that the Apostle John would send, Diotrephes would also prevent them from receiving these people. Furthermore, he spoke malicious words against John and his leadership; and John promised to deal with him when he came to visit the church.

Now, in this small book, John mentions a few names of the members of that church. If they were not members of that church, probably he would not have known their names; and would not have been able to deal with the problems that they had. While we are on this point, let me just say that the Diotrephes spirit is very much alive in our Modern Day church. It is the kind of spirit that does not recognize the authority of the pastor or leader. It is the kind of spirit that always objects to what the leader says; even if it is right. If the leader does not consult some people about decisions to be made, then they try to disrupt the plan. Yes! They are in many churches; and many times it is the greatest hindrance to the progress of the church. The Diotrephes spirit has to be dealt with in accordance with the Word of God.

In some of Paul's letters to the churches, he gave a long list of people. Sometimes he talks about people who were backslidden, those who forsook him at other times, and he spoke about people who are doing well in the church. I am saying this to say that Paul knew the members of the church. That's the reason why he could have called them by their names, and the reason he knew when they were missing or had backslidden.

The Officers Of The Church

Pastors

The church of Jesus Christ is organized. There are various officers in the church whose job descriptions are given in the Bible. We have established that God works through leadership; His works are in order. The Holy Spirit brings order. The Scripture says in *1Corinthians 14:40*, *"Let all things be done decently and in order"*. God has given the order as to how things must be done in His church. We read in *1Timothy3:1*, *"This is a true saying, if a man desires the office of a bishop, he desireth a good work"*. Here it is talking about pastors or overseers. Then, in *verse 8* it says, *"Likewise must the deacons be grave, not doubled tongue, not given to much wine; not greedy of filthy lucre"*.

Deacons are servants who assist the pastors in the work of the church and in particular, the material aspects such as visitation and serving tables (that's what the Bible calls it). Whereas, the pastor's main duty is to feed the flock spiritually. So, he must spend quality time in prayer, getting direction from God, preparing himself to meet the spiritual needs of the church and the community, and allowing God to speak to his spirit on behalf of the church and community. Also he should spend quality time studying the Word that the congregation would be well fed spiritually.

In the book of **Acts 6:1-4** we read, *"And in those days, when the number of the disciples was multiplied, there arose a murmuring of the Grecians against the Hebrews, because their widows were neglected in the daily ministration. Then the twelve called the multitude of the disciples unto them and said: it is not reason that we should leave the word of God and serve tables. Wherefore brethren, look ye out among you seven men of honest report, full of the Holy Ghost and wisdom, whom we may appoint over this business. But we will give ourselves continually to prayer and to the ministry of the word"*.

I am of the opinion that if pastors were spending quality time in prayer and the word of God like the apostles of old, and the deacons were sticking to their role the church would be more effective in this world. The pastor must pray, study, teach the Word and also manage the church of God. The Bible says in **1Timothy 5:17**, *"Let the elders who rule well be counted worthy of double honor, especially they who labor in word and doctrine"*.

Let me use some other Scriptures to establish the point that the pastor is the ruler under God in the local church; although some people don't support this view. Paul writing to Titus (a pastor) said to him in **Titus 1:5**, *" For this cause left I thee in Crete, that thou shouldest set in order the things that are* *wanting, and ordain elders in every city, as I had appointed thee"*. Titus was placed in the church by the apostle Paul, and part of his duty was to put things in proper order in the church. He had to deal with unruly people, those teaching false doctrines and the immoral.

In the book of **Hebrews 13:7** we read, *"Remember them which have the rule over you, who have spoken unto you the word of God; whose faith follow, considering the end of their conversation"*. In verse **17** it says, *"obey them that have the rule over you, and submit yourselves: for they watch for your souls, as they that must give account, that they may do it with joy, and not with grief: for that is unprofitable for you"*. We are living in an age where people don't like to submit to authority; so they try to get away from the concept of authority in the church. But God has set pastors in His church as the authoritative figure over the church.

Before I move from this aspect of the pastor as God's set man over the church, let us look at a few more Scriptures to make it abundantly clear to all. Because, if we don't know who the leader is, then we may have many heads, and anything with several heads reminds me of a monster. Paul talking about a bishop, elder or pastor says in **1Timothy.3:4 - 5**, *"One that ruleth well his own house, having his children in subjection with all gravity. For if a man know not how to rule his own house, how shall he take care of the church of God?"* So, the pastor must be a good example in his own house, a good ruler of his home - because part of his duty over the church is to rule and if he cannot rule his own house, then he is disqualified to rule God's house which is the local church here in this passage.

In the book of **Acts 20:28**, Paul speaking to the pastors of the churches at Ephesus says, *"Take heed therefore unto yourselves, and to all the flock, over the which the Holy Ghost hath made you overseers, to feed the church of God, which he hath purchased with his own blood"*. Again we see leaders as having oversight. In the New Testament, the most common words used to refer to the pastoral position is the word "elder", but now the word pastor is more popular. In the Old Testament, the word "pastor" was also used to refer to the leader over the people of God; and may I say God was very hard with the pastors who did not rule in His fear. This is what the Old Testament says about unfaithful pastors, and I believe these words remain true to the pastors of the day who would be unfaithful to the Word and the flock of God.

We read in **Jeremiah 23:1**, *"Woe be unto the pastors that destroy and scatter the sheep of my pasture, saith the Lord"*. These are strong words against any pastor who feels that since God has given him the rule over His church, he can treat the flock of God as he wishes. These woes from Jeremiah were to the priests and false prophets who fed themselves, while the people of God scattered or went into captivity.

Deacons

Maybe in the Old Testament, the only helpers would be the Levites; who would help the priest in the work of the Tabernacle. We have seen that the same qualifications is required for both pastor and deacon according to **1Timothy 3**, except that it did not say that the deacons must be apt to teach; and I believe this is because it is part of the pastor's job to teach the people and not necessarily the deacons. The Scripture says that the deacons must not be greedy for money. Maybe, part of their function had to do with church funds. Maybe, they were involved in the administrative work of the church depending on the gift they had.

The Deacons are chosen from among the congregation to help the pastor meet the needs of the congregation. However, the pastor might be chosen from another congregation, or from overseas to pastor a church he may not even know; the Counsel of Elders who would be foremost in the appointment of a pastor would have some knowledge about that pastor. And the church that counsels – which is supposed to be Spirit Filled men, must choose that individual after they have prayed and are sure that he is the person God wants them to put in authority over that particular church. So those deacons don't have to leave their jobs to serve the church, it is just additional work they have to do for the Lord.

Apostles In The Church

This position and that of the Prophet is greatly debated in the church today. Are there apostles today? Let us first look at the twelve apostles of the Lord. What does the Word say about them and are there any more like them? The twelve apostles that the Lord chose – there are no more like them in that specific sense because they lived and worked with Him on earth and were chosen by the Lord Jesus Christ himself who said to them literally "come and follow me". They are called twelve apostles and it seems that this number was of specific significance to the Lord. So when Judas betrayed the Son of

God and committed suicide, there was need for someone else to fill the void that was there. So, they chose Matthias.

This story is found in Acts chapter one. Again, we read in **Acts 2:14**, *"But Peter, standing up with the eleven, lifted up his voice and said unto them, ye men of Judaea and all ye that dwell at Jerusalem, be this known unto you, and hearken to my words"*.

Although there were about a hundred and twenty believers, the Bible says "Peter standing up with the eleven". So, he was the spokesman for the other eleven apostles, of whom Matthias is now recognized as one of the twelve. So the number twelve was a fixed number for those who were there when Jesus walked among them. To me, the book of Revelation sets the seal on this matter about the original twelve apostles (Judas not included). **Revelation 21:14** says, *"And the wall of the city had twelve foundations, and in them the names of the twelve apostles of the Lamb"*. These twelve had a special place on earth and even in the New Heaven and New Earth.

We know, however, that apart from these twelve Apostles there were other Apostles in the New Testament who, I believe, could be in the Body of Christ today. This is what I would like to look into at this moment. The book of **Ephesians 4:11-14** (referring to the gifted men God gave to His church) says, *"And he gave some apostles, and some prophets and some evangelists; and some pastors and teachers. For the perfecting of the saints, for the work of ministry, for the edifying of the body of Christ: Till we all come in the unity of the faith, and of the knowledge of the Son of God, unto a perfect man, unto the measure of the stature of the fullness of Christ. That we* *henceforth be no more children, tossed to and fro, and carried about with every wind of doctrine, by the sleight of men, and cunning craftiness whereby they lie in wait to deceive".*

You cannot find a clearer text on the matter concerning apostles. This text states clearly, without a shadow of a doubt that Jesus gave apostles to His church; among many other ministries. If the Bible says He gave them to the church, as long as the church is here, we will have apostles, prophets and all the others.

But here is the hypocrisy of some Bible teachers. They will agree that this verse of Scripture is infallible; but what some of them would do is misinterpret the Scriptures. That same verse (vs.11) which talks about apostles, prophets, evangelists, pastors and teachers, that Jesus gave to His church; they will say we still have evangelists, pastors and teachers today but no apostles and prophets. I say this is being dishonest to the text of God's Word; just to defend our denominational stand on the matter and the Lord is not pleased with it.

Furthermore, the text gives the duration for which we shall have them. It states, "Till we all come in the unity of the faith and of the knowledge of the Son of God, unto a perfect man; unto the measure of the stature of the fullness of Christ". Have we arrived there as yet? No! And as long as we are here, we will be striving for perfection. God has given His church these gifted men to help us in our daily Christian walk, and to do the work of the ministry. This is what the Bible says, and I choose to obey God rather than man.

These gifted men are there for the perfecting of the saints, for the work of the ministry, for the edifying of the Body of Christ. The church is not perfect as yet, and these gifted ministers (every one of them), help to perfect the saints. As long as the church is here on earth, it will have work to do. These ministers are there to help the church do the work of the ministry by their teaching, by the different gifts God has given to them, and by their personal examples - they teach the church what is to be done.

The text also says that they are there to edify the church. When will the church not need edifying? Certainly as long as it is on earth it would need edifying. Therefore, it will need apostles to be involved in the process of edification. The Bible says also that these gifted men have been given to the church that they will help stabilize the church: *"That we henceforth be no more children tossed to and fro, and carried about with every wind of doctrine, by the sleight of men and cunning craftiness, whereby they lie in wait to deceive"*. So, these men are there in the Body of Christ to help the church go in the right direction to take the right course. God has given them special ability to discern and wisdom to know what to do in difficult situations.

We remember the story in the book of *Acts 15* about whether or not the brethren should keep the Law of Moses and be circumcised. When the local leaders could not handle the problem, they brought it to the apostles to have the final say. There are and will be difficult situations in the church, and at times we need the apostles to help give direction. I believe when pastors falter at times, disciplinary actions need to be taken, the church should not handle these matters. The apostles should.

Again, we see in the book of *Acts 8* that Phillip, an evangelist, went down to the city of Samaria, and preached with great success as many were converted and baptized. He realized that he had done his part, so he went to the apostles and handed to them, those who were newly converted. The apostles Peter and John came to them and were able to establish them stronger in the faith and to deal with what was not Phillip's area of ministry. The patterns are in the Scripture and we must follow God's pattern in His church.

There are lots of churches that are becoming museums in many parts of the world, especially in Europe. Many countries where the gospel once flourished, and where there were many revivals and many Christians, have many big church buildings today but few Christians. Why? It is because they have forsaken the way of the Lord. They do not want apostles and prophets in the church. Their brilliance and technology has replaced the gifted men and women of God in the church, which is now being governed by "worldly wise men" rather than spiritually anointed men. Their worldly wisdom cannot fight the devil and prevail; as a result, the church is declining daily in some parts of the world.

The prophet Jeremiah puts it in the right perspective when he says in *Jeremiah 2:13*, *"For my people hath committed two evils; they have forsaken me the fountain of living waters, and hewed them out cisterns, broken cisterns that can hold no water"*. The church needs to go back to the New Testament, to see how God structured His church and follow that pattern humbly and willingly.

We read that the Corinthian church had lots of problems. It seems that they had problems with every thing – they even had problems with communion. Whosoever was leading the church could not handle the problems. They even went to the Law for each other. What a mess that church was in – a man was even living with his father's wife. But the apostle Paul helped solve these problems in the church. When you have problems like these in a church, and you don't have gifted men whom God has given to the church to come in and give direction, many times that particular assembly or church becomes a laughing stock in the eyes of the community.

Also, throughout the New Testament, we see the apostles starting new churches in different parts of the world; especially Barnabas and Paul. After they established these churches, they put structures in place and moved on. Many times, they came back to visit and to strengthen the brethren. This is still part of the work of the apostles today. Some of the people we call missionaries are truly apostles but I don't know why we are afraid to call them what the Bible calls them.

There is absolutely no doubt that there were other apostles apart from the twelve whose uniqueness we have shown. Certainly, we know that Paul was an apostle, but the Bible shows that there were others also. In the book of *Acts 14:14* we read, *"Which when the apostles, Barnabas and Paul, heard of, they rent their clothes, and ran in among the people, crying out"*. So this verse is clearly saying that Barnabas was an apostle as well as Paul, because it reads, *"when the apostles"*.

Again, we have James, the Lord's brother, being called an apostle. He was not one of the original twelve apostles - the James's we read about as apostles are James the son of Zebedee, *(Matthew20: 20-24)* whom King Herod killed with the sword in *Acts 12*, and James the son of Alphaeus whom we read about in *Acts 1: 13*.

But later, we see James the Lord's brother, who was not in the days of the Lord Jesus on earth, being called an apostle. He probably was not even saved until the end of the Lord's ministry on earth. *John 7:5* says, *"For neither did his brethren believe in him"*. In *Galatians 1:19,* we see James, the Lord's brother, being called an apostle. This is what the text says, *"But other of the apostles saw I none, save James, the Lord's brother"*. So, the only apostle that he saw was James the Lord's brother, who was not of the original twelve apostles.

In the book of *1Thessalonians 2:6,* we read about the other apostles apart from the original twelve. This is what we read, *"Nor of men sought we glory, neither of you, nor yet of others, when we might have been burdensome as the apostles of Christ"*. It is obvious that Paul was referring to the men who were with him at that time and we are sure that Silvanus was with him as well as Timotheus because chapter *1:1* says so. Therefore, it is reasonable to believe that what he is referring to in chapter *2:6* are these two whom he called apostles also.

Some people say that Paul said that he was the last apostle. Are they right? No, not at all. This is the verse they use when making this statement but let us hear what the verse says for itself. *1Corinthians 15: 8-9* reads, *"And last of all he was seen of me also, as of one born out of due time. For I am the least of the apostles, that am not meet to be called an apostle, because I persecuted the church of God"*. Now this is talking about the different groups of people that the Lord appeared to after his resurrection. Paul says, "last of all he was seen of me also". He is basically saying he was the last to see the resurrected Lord. He also said that he was the least of the apostles, not the last - he put himself as least because he said before that he persecuted the church of Christ. So, he feels as if God should not have chosen him. But, this is not of works - it is about the grace of God.

Let me close with this Scripture found in *1Corinthians 12:28*: *"And God hath set some in the church; first apostles, secondarily prophets, thirdly teachers, after that miracles, then gifts of healings, helps, governments, diversities of tongues"*. It is God who sets up His church, and He placed apostles first in His church. Why should we try to destroy what God has placed in His church? If we do so we will weaken the church. Let the church be the church. Let us allow the gifted apostles to function in the church. As a matter of fact, they are supposed to be the head under God in the church.

Prophets In The Church

We have already looked at the text in **Ephesians 4:11**, which says that the prophet is a gift of ministry that God has given to His church: so we are sure that God wants the prophet in the church just as He wants the evangelist, pastor and teacher. As a matter of fact, the prophet is second only to the apostle.

Acts 13:1-3 reads, *"Now there were in the church that was at Antioch certain prophets and teachers; as Barnabas and Simeon that was called Niger, and Lucius of Cyrene, and Manaen, which had been brought up with Herod the tetrarch, and Saul. As they ministered to the Lord, and fasted, the Holy Ghost said, separate me Barnabas and Saul for the work whereunto I have called them. And when they had fasted and prayed, and laid their hands on them, they sent them away"*.

We see in the early church (which is the pattern we should be following), that there were prophets who spoke forth the word of God concerning what God wanted Paul and Barnabas to do at that particular time. And the church laid hands on them and prayed for them since the Christians knew that they

51

were going by divine direction. Therefore, how can we say that these things are no longer of any significance in the church of the living God?

The prophet is one who speaks forth on behalf of another, so God uses specific persons in His church to speak on His behalf. He speaks through these individuals. These words are not of the same level as Scripture; for we read in *2 Peter 1:19*, *"We have also a more sure word of prophecy; whereunto ye do well that ye take heed, as unto a light that shineth in a dark place, until the day dawn and the day star arise in your hearts"*.

So, the prophecies of today cannot take the place of the Scripture, but God uses prophets to speak to their local churches or to their nations concerning what God wants any particular group of people to hear at any time. For example, we read in *Acts 11:27-29*, *"And in those days came prophets from Jerusalem unto Antioch. And there stood up one of them named Agabus, and signified by the Spirit that there should be great death throughout all the world: which came to pass in the days of Claudius Caesar. Then the disciples, every man according to his ability determined to send relief unto the brethren which dwelt in Judea"*.

Here, we see the prophet prophesied of the famine to come in Judea. This helped the church to get ready and because they were prepared, it did not take them by surprise. There were prophets in the church who told them what was going to happen. My dear friends, we need all the gifted men and ministers of God in the church today, as we had in the early church.

Giving & The Church

Tithe: The Principle of Putting God First

This is not a matter without question in the church. Questions such as: "Is this for the New Testament church?" "Was this not just under the Law?" and many more, are questions that we will try to answer from the Word.

What is a tithe?

A tithe is ten percent of your gross income; which you give to the House of God to support His work. But before going into the nitty-gritty of tithing, let us first look at the principle of putting God first. Now the Scriptures make it abundantly clear that we must put God first in all that we do. In *Matthew 6:33* Jesus says, *"But seek ye first the Kingdom of God and his righteousness, and all these things shall be added unto you"*. The things that He promised us that shall be added are things like clothing, food, health and all these other things that we are so concerned about. The bills, the loans, building our homes and having our own cars – Jesus says that if we put Him first, He will take care of us. So, with our monies we must put God first. We must give Him what He demands before taking care of the bills, and He will take care of us.

One of the problems we have today is that we try to take care of everything and give God the rest; but God doesn't deserve crumbs at our hands. He is our Maker, Lord and King; therefore, we must treat Him as such. Even the heathen who serve false gods – gods made by man's hands, make sure they bring their best offering to their gods. The thing that you love, you spend on it. Have you not noticed that some athletes spend thousands of dollars on their gears? Some people spend thousands of dollars a day gambling, and many times they lose – yet they keep on spending. Others spend thousands of dollars drinking at the bar in one day; and if you were to ask them why they are wasting all this money drinking liquor, you would hear responses like – "its my money. I worked for it".

In the Christian life, we must be addicted to God. Everything we do must be for His glory and honor, and we must give to further His cause. By the way, the more we give to His cause, the more He gives back to us. I have seen people who are addicted to illegal drugs being very hungry – almost starving and you give them five dollars and the first thing they will get is some more drugs; and if there is any money left then they will buy something to eat. When we really love God, we put Him first in everything; and if He is not first in our money, it is most likely He is not first in our lives.

Let us look at Judas, one of the twelve apostles of Jesus for a moment. He went out with the others, so you would have thought that all was well with him. However, Judas' greatest problem was that he loved money, and he did not want to spend it on Christ. He thought spending money on Christ was a waste. Let us read the account in *John 12:3*-6; *"Then took Mary a pound of ointment of spikenard, very costly, and anointed the feet of Jesus, and wiped his feet with her hair: and the house was filled with the odour of the ointment. Then saith one of his disciples Judas Iscariot, Simon's son which should betray him; why was not this ointment sold for three hundred pence, and given to the poor? This he said, not that he cared for the poor; but because he was a thief, and had the bag, and bare what was put therein"*.

If God is not Lord over your money, He is not Lord over your soul. We all know what became of Judas. He sold Jesus for thirty pieces of silver, yet he never got to enjoy that money: that same money tormented him. You can never be free as a child of God when you are robbing Him of that which He demands from you.

Why should one find giving ten percent from his income to God's house such a hard thing? Personally I don't know why; because to me, if you don't give, you deprive your own self from receiving God's abundant blessings. It is God who gives you everything that you have in the first place: the job you have, the education, the talent, health etc. And you know what? He can withdraw it when He wants: or, you can have all these things and yet not be happy. Why should we behave as greedy unlearnt little children with God when all that we have is from God?

Let us hear what King David says about this matter as he prepares to make a great sacrifice to God in *1Chronicles 29:12 - 15.* *"Both riches and honor come of thee; and thou reignest over all, and in thine hand is power and might; and in thine hand it is to make great and to give strength unto all. Now therefore, our God, we thank thee and praise thy glorious name. But who am I, and what is my people that we should be able to offer so willingly after this sort? For all things come of thee and of thine own have we given thee. For we are strangers before thee, and sojourners, as were all our fathers: our days on the earth are as a shadow, and there is none abiding".*

God is the owner of everything; therefore, if He asks us to return one tenth of what He has given to us, that should not be a problem. Really and truly it is not ours and we are all strangers on earth since nothing here belongs to us. So we must lay down treasures in our home in heaven and give to further the Kingdom of God. Now let's get back to the unlearned, greedy child. If that child's father bought him chocolate every week and each week that child should leave one chunk for his dad but refuses to give it to him, would you not call this child greedy and unlearnt; because this child doesn't even realize that his father is the source, and if he decides to be stingy with the father, the father can be stingy with him also.

My dear friends, on the matter of giving, let us not be like children tossed to and fro. Let us be committed to paying our tithes more than being committed to paying our electricity bill; because the supplier (who is God) can cut our supply.

The difference perhaps is when God disconnects you no man can connect you; and at times He disconnects you everywhere.

My advice to you is that you pay your tithes no matter what, and God will take care of everything else. Remember, God must be first. Let us look at this principle from the Old Testament with Cain and Abel: the first boys who ever lived. In **Genesis 4:1 -8**, we see the principle of putting God first in respect to giving or could we say the principle of tithing although the word is not used. It reads, *"And Adam knew Eve his wife; and she conceived and bare Cain, and said, I have begotten a man from the Lord. And she again bare his brother Abel. And Abel was a keeper of sheep, but Cain was a tiller of the ground.*

And in the process of time, it came to pass that Cain brought of the fruit of the ground an offering unto the Lord. And Abel, he also brought of the firstlings of his flock and of the fat thereof. And the Lord had respect unto Abel and to his offering: but unto Cain and to his offering he had not respect. And Cain was very wroth, and his countenance fell. And the Lord said unto Cain; Why art thou wroth? And why is thy countenance fallen? If thou doest well, shall thou not be accepted? And if thou doest not well, sin lieth at the door. And unto thee shall be his desire, and thou shall rule over him. And Cain talked with Abel his brother; and it came to pass, when they were in the field, that Cain rose up against Abel his brother, and slew him".

Here, we have a great story about giving to God what is expected. On the other hand; a brother from the same house withholds from God what was required. Let us be reminded that this Scripture is taken from Genesis chapter four; and this was the first family on earth. This was not under the Law, and this was way before the flood. So, from the first family that God created, we observe the principle of giving to God a specific kind of offering was taught. We also see here that it is not just any kind of offering will do. There is an acceptable offering to God and an un-acceptable one. The Scripture says, "And the Lord had respect unto Abel and to his offering, but unto Cain and his offering he had not respect". It would seem that the way we treat God at the offering table really says who we are. God had no respect for Cain and his offering. Does God have any respect for you and your offering? Does He take delight in what you give to Him? Because Abel gave God what was required of him, God blessed him abundantly, whereas Cain was not doing well, and it all started at the offering table.

The matter of giving in the church is a serious one. Some pastors don't like to talk about it because of the attitude of the members. Once it is money talk, they begin to grumble and murmur. These are those who have picked up that Cain spirit; but the pastors and teachers must speak about tithing in church because it is a very important doctrine in the Bible. And like Cain, a lot of families are not doing well because of how they treat God at the offering table.

Cain had a spirit of vexation in him; do you know why? It was because he saw his brother doing better than he was. It was so terrible that God had to come down and talk to Cain about the matter. God said, "Why art thou wroth? And why is thy countenance fallen?" There are thousands of people in our churches today whom God is talking to about giving to Him. But like Cain, no matter what means He uses, they will not change. He will speak through books, preaching, dreams and visions. He will even send angels to some, but they will not change. However, I have met people who after they heard the word of God on giving, began practicing it; and their whole life changed – both spiritually and financially. The Cain spirit left and the Abel spirit came. The devourer left and the windows of heaven opened to them. Don't argue about giving – be like Abel. Give God that which He requires and over. Never be stingy with God. Always give God over and above.

Unfortunately, in spite of the fact God Himself spoke to Cain about his giving and promised to bless him if he did well, Cain still did not change. Don't be like Cain. Now we observe from the text that the first murder committed in the Bible was over money. Or should we say over giving the best to God. Because Abel gave a more acceptable offering to God than Cain and God blessed him, Cain got jealous and killed his own brother. All he had to do was give like his brother. Give God the best that he had. Change his view on giving. Try something different. Obey God. Instead, he loved what he had more than God. He put himself before God; therefore, he opened the door to the devil. We can let the devil have an opening in our lives through the way we value money. Eve refused to obey God and the devil gave her other ideas. If you don't want to obey God in giving Him what is required, the devil will give you other ideas.

Friends, what and how we give to God are very important and it has been so from the beginning. Adam must have taught his family about giving God their best not the rejected, but the fattest and nicest. Not scraps or leftovers but the very best that you have. The best belongs to the Blesser! Now, let us turn our attention to the New Testament for a moment to see how money can be a barrier, which can prevent us from entering the Kingdom of heaven.

In *Luke 18:18 - 24*; we have a rich young man asking Jesus for instructions about how to enter the Kingdom of heaven or how to have eternal life. It reads, *"And a certain ruler asked him saying; Good master, what shall I do to inherit eternal life? And Jesus said unto him, why callest thou me good? None is good, save one, that's God. Thou knowest the commandments; Do not commit adultery; Do not kill, Do not steal, Do not bear false witness, Honor thy father and mother. And he said, all these have I kept from my youth up. Now when Jesus heard these things he said unto him, yet lackest thou one thing: sell all that thou hast and distribute unto the poor, and thou shall have treasure in heaven; and come follow me. And when he heard this, he was very sorrowful; for he was rich. And when Jesus saw that he was very sorrowful; he said, how hardly shall they that have riches enter into the Kingdom of God".*

This man wanted to have eternal life. He kept all the commandments; yet, he was under bondage to money. Jesus was not Lord over his money. He walked away very sorrowful because he did not have the right perspective about money. His attitude hindered him from having eternal life. We must obey God in everything including our money. If He is Lord over our lives He must be Lord over our monies also.

Tithing & The Church

Some people say they don't believe in tithing because it was under the Law. I trust that by now you have realized that this is false, because we have already seen that from Cain and Abel. The principle of giving God our best had been established; but now we want to look at the root of tithing in the Scriptures. Who first started tithing? Surely, it was not Moses. Guess who: Abraham. So tithing started four hundred and thirty years before the Law. When I use the word "tithe" I mean the principle of giving God ten percent. Because we saw Abel giving God an acceptable offering way before that; and I believe that was much more than ten percent, if we understand the description of sacrifice properly. Abraham was four hundred and thirty years before the Law according to the Scriptures. *Galatians 3:17* says, *"And this I say, that the covenant that was confirmed before of God in Christ, the Law which was four hundred and thirty years after, cannot disannul, that it should make the promise of none effect"*.

Just as the promise of salvation preceded the Law, so tithing preceded the Law. Tithing started with Abraham and not with Moses. Why is this important? It is important because this same Abraham is the father of the faithful. The Bible says all those who are of faith are the children of Abraham. So, just as Abraham taught us justification by faith so he taught us tithing as children of God. As we read *Genesis 14:20*, we realize for the first time the word "tithe" is mentioned in the Bible. Let us be reminded that this is not in Exodus, Leviticus, Numbers or Deuteronomy. Moses' grandfather had not yet been born, much less Moses. This is what the text says; *"And blessed be the most high God, which hath delivered thine enemies into thy hand; and he gave him tithes of all"*. This was after Abraham re-captured Lot from the enemy. In reality, Melchezedek met him, and had communion with him; and there, Abraham paid tithe of all that he had to God.

I believe that showing gratitude to God for blessing him made him successful and gave him victory over the enemy. This practice of tithing continued from then on. It moved from before the Law to under the Law and after the Law, as we will see later on in this chapter. When Jacob was running away from his brother and had that great vision from God: a ladder set up on the earth with the top reaching heaven and the Lord standing above it. He vowed a vow unto the Lord, and part of this vow was that he would pay his tithe. When there is true repentance or conversion, paying our tithes is one of the things we do.

Let me quote a portion of Scripture about tithes under the Law. Now there are many such Scriptures under the Law. In **Leviticus 27:30 - 34** we read, *"And all the tithe of the land, whether of the seed of the land, or of the fruit of the tree, is the Lord's: it is holy unto the Lord. And if a man will at all redeem ought of his tithes, he shall add thereto the fifth part thereof. And concerning the tithe of the herd or of the flock, even of whatsoever passeth under the rod, the tenth shall be holy unto the Lord. He shall not search whether it be good or bad; neither shall he change it. And if he changes it at all, both it and the change thereof shall be holy; it shall not be redeemed"*. We recognize that God was very strict about His tenth. Under the Law you could not even exchange it. Whatsoever passed through your hand, you had to pay tithe from it. It was something holy unto the Lord, and only to the Lord was it to be used.

In the book of Haggai, we have the story of the children of Israel returning from captivity. They laid the foundation of the temple and the work ceased. The people had no more desire to build the house of God. They were not giving towards the project. As a matter of fact, they said it was not time to build the house of the Lord – yet they were building their own houses. God was totally displeased with them, and sent His prophet to rebuke them for the way they viewed His house, and for putting themselves before Him in their giving.

This is what the text says in *Haggai 1:2 – 11:*

"Thus speaketh the Lord of hosts saying; these people say, the time is not come, that the Lord's house should be built. Then came the word of the Lord by Haggai the prophet saying, it is time for you, O ye, to dwell in your ceiled houses, and this house lie waste? Now therefore thus saith the Lord of host; consider your ways. Ye have sown much, and bring in little, ye eat and have not enough; ye drink but ye are not filled with drink, ye clothe you, but there is none warm; and he that earneth wages, earneth wages to put it into a bag with holes. Thus saith the Lord of host, consider your ways. Go up to the mountain, and bring wood and build the house; and I will take pleasure in it, and I will be glorified; saith the Lord. Ye looked for much, and lo, it came to little; and when ye brought it home, I did blow upon it. Why? Saith the Lord of host; because of mine house that is waste, and ye run every man unto his own house. Therefore the heaven over you is stayed from dew, and the earth is stayed from her fruit; and I called for a drought upon the land, and upon the mountains, and upon the corn, and upon the new wine, and upon the oil, and upon

that which the ground bringeth forth, and upon men, and upon cattle, and upon all the labor of the hands".

These people had the wrong attitude towards giving to the things of God. Yet, they were doing their best to improve themselves. But God sent a prophet to ask them to consider their behavior towards giving to the house of God. The prophet told them that they had been sowing much to try to improve themselves and yet their efforts had been disappointing.

They sowed much to themselves, but they received little. Why? Because they had forgotten God in their giving. They had not sown toward the house of God - only to themselves. Therefore, God was not prospering their efforts. They were eating but not being filled, drinking but still thirsty, clothed yet there was no warmth.

They were trying to save money, but it was like putting it in a bag with holes. Why was this happening to them? Because of the way they treated the house of God. It was as if their whole lives were under a curse - and indeed they were cursed by God Himself because they did not give to His house the way that they should. They were being stingy with God; so God was being stingy with them likewise. God said that they should build a house which He would take pleasure in. When we give to see the church of the Lord Jesus advance, He takes pleasure in it. God closes up heaven upon the person who will not give to His house: there shall be no rain upon your seeds and no rain upon your efforts. There will not be blessings but curses.

Harvest is always disappointing to the man who does not give to God what is required. Even when his harvest is plentiful, it breeds worms. The end is disappointing; his goal cannot be realized. He will work hard and die poor unless he changes his mind concerning giving to the house of God. We cannot be in covenant with God and not walk in accordance with His Word. No! It shall not be well with you. The way to get much from God is to give much to God. Any man who gives to God his best with the right attitude will likewise get the best from God. The good thing about this passage in Haggai is that when the Lord spoke to the people through his prophet they took heed of the message. They realized that they were going wrong and they repented, and God blessed them and their household.

Let us now turn our attention to the book of Malachi for a short while. Let us be reminded that this was a people who had dishonored God in every respect, but because of our study, we will limit it to their un-faithfulness in giving to God. *Malachi 1: 7-8* says, *"Ye offer polluted bread upon mine altar: and ye say wherein have we polluted thee? In that ye say; the table of the Lord is contemptible. And if ye offer the blind for sacrifice, is it not evil? And if ye offer the lame and the sick, is it not evil? Offer it now unto thy governor; will he be pleased with thee, or accept thy person? saith the Lord of Hosts"*. Here, we see the people offering to God what was polluted and rejected. This is exactly how some church folks treat God today. We give to God what we do not want.

The people brought blind animals to be sacrificed to the Lord. Oh! What a dishonor to God. They brought animals that were sick, which they could not give to their Governors or Prime

Ministers. These, they brought to the King of Kings and Lord of Lords. Can you imagine bringing a blind sacrifice to the Lord; or bringing a sick animal to God as a sacrifice? Why is it that some people think that they should give God only the rejected stuff?

Let us read **Malachi 3: 8-12**; which says, *"Will a man rob God? Yet ye have robbed me: but say wherein have we robbed thee? In tithes and offerings; ye are cursed with a curse: for ye have robbed me, even this whole nation. Bring ye all the tithes into the storehouse, that there may be meat in mine house; and prove me now herewith saith the Lord of host: if I will not open you the windows of heaven and pour you out a blessing, that there will not be room enough to receive it; and I will rebuke the devourer for your sakes, and he shall not destroy the fruits of your ground neither shall your vine cast her fruit before the time in the field, saith the Lord of host. And all nations shall call you blessed: for ye shall be a delightsome land, saith the Lord of host".*

The question is: "Will a man rob God?" Maybe if this text were not in the Word, we would be tempted to say that we can never rob God. But, we cannot run away from the truth – man can, and has, is robbing and will rob God. Now to me, this is very serious. I think of it as the greatest robbery that can ever be committed. This is worse than robbing a Bank and escaping with billions of dollars. This is not like robbing the biggest financial markets on earth. This is robbing God! To rob is to take that which belongs to someone else. So people rob God by taking His tithe and using it for something else or on them selves. No matter what your excuse is you are guilty because nowhere in the Word did God tell you to use it for something else. As a matter of fact, He says, "Bring ye all the tithes into the storehouse" and by "all" He means all.

Do you know He sees you and He knows what you do with His money? And He says it shall never prosper you. You need to repent, and start paying your tithe from this very moment. The Bible says those who rob God are cursed with a curse; not just any curse. God Himself curses them. You can turn away and ask Him to remove that curse which only He can remove, after you have repented and started to pay your tithe. In the modern church, a lot of people want to be blessed, especially in the area of finance, and so they come to the servant of God and ask him to pray for them and the minister would pray. Yet these people's situations do not improve. Not because of a lack of faith, but because these people are not standing right in the sight of God.

The pastor may see them as great church members, the government may see them as great citizens, but if they are not paying their tithes, God sees them as thieves. They should be locked up, but they go to the altar as if all is well. The pastor cannot pray blessings upon such persons. These people need to change their attitude toward giving, and when they do, God will open the prison door and set them free.

When we pay our tithe, God promises to open the windows of heaven and pour us out blessings that there will not be room enough to receive them. And it does not matter where you live, if you put God first, He will put you first. He will sustain you in famine. He did it for the prophets of old, He provided for Israel forty years in the desert – so He can provide for you wherever you are.

Now, the Word says if we pay our tithes God will rebuke the devourer for our sake; but, if we don't pay our tithes the devourer will devour our crops, our children, our finances, our health, and our families, and cause us to spend money. However, if we pay our tithes, God will provide security for us. We cannot rob God and expect Him to protect us. He will allow the devourer to enter our homes, but if we turn to Him with our whole hearts and pay our tithes, God Himself will rebuke the devourer for our sakes. There is protection for those who pay their tithes and live holy lives. Some people say that the New Testament does not talk about paying tithe; therefore, they have no obligation to pay tithes. But they are wrong! We read in **Matthew 23:23**, *"Woe unto the scribes and Pharisees; hypocrites. For ye pay tithe of mint and anise and cumin, and have omitted the weightier matters of the law, judgment, mercy and faith: these ought ye to have done, and not to leave the other undone"*.

Of course, Jesus was pronouncing woes upon the Scribes and Pharisees in this portion of Scripture. But let us look at the Scripture carefully. Jesus says that they were doing well. He recognized that they tried to pay tithes of every little thing; but the weightier matters of the Law they left out or did not place emphasis on. Jesus was saying that we should both pay our tithes, and seek to have judgment, mercy and faith. He says we ought to pay our tithe, but we should also include the others: "these ought ye to have done, and not to leave the others undone".

The others that were undone were judgment, mercy and faith. You see, my brothers and sisters, we cannot do what we feel like doing in the church of the living God and omit what we want. No! We must be faithful to the Word. Without a shadow of a doubt, this portion of Scripture is teaching that we should pay tithe.

Jesus condemned the Pharisees and scribes for almost everything but not about tithe. They were faithful in this regard.

And although they were probably going to end up in hell because they did not do all the other things that were necessary for salvation such as: accepting Jesus Christ as the only Savior of the world and being born again, one thing we are sure about that they did right, is that they paid their tithes. And it is believed that the Scribes and Pharisees were among the richest people in Israel. Could this be because they observed this biblical principle? Or, once you give God His part, He will open the windows of heaven and pour you out blessings that there will not be room enough to receive them? They knew God was not a man who would lie. Whatsoever He says, He will do. God is bound by His word. Or in essence, God keeps His word.

Luke *18: 10 - 14* reads, *"Two men went up into the temple to pray: the one a Pharisee and the other a publican. The Pharisee stood and prayed thus with himself: God, I thank thee that I am not as other men are; extortioners, unjust, adulterers, or even as this publican. I fast twice in the week, I give tithes of all that I possess. And the publican, standing afar off; would not lift so much his eyes unto heaven, but smote upon his breast saying, God be merciful to me a sinner. I tell you, this man went to his house justified rather than the other. For everyone that exalteth himself shall be abased; and he that humbleth himself shall be exalted.*" In this parable, Jesus gives us the attitude of two men: one who is self-righteous, proud, and trusted in his good works; such as paying tithes of all that he had and fasting twice a week; and the other man who feels that he is unworthy and, seeks the mercy of God. He confessed his sins, and humbled himself before God.

The Bible says he went home justified; whereas the man who boasted about his fasting and giving of tithes of all that he had went home un-justified. God did not justify the publican for not paying his tithe - No! But because he recognized that he had sinned, he asked God to forgive him, which Jesus did. Maybe one of the sins he realized he had committed was that of not paying his tithe. I believe from that day onward he was changed. You see, the matter here is not about tithing or fasting being wrong, neither is God justifying sin; but showing mercy to those who would come before him in repentance - and the proud He sends away empty. We cannot earn our way to heaven by our giving; but those who are on their way to heaven will recognize that part of the Law after you are saved is that there are things that accompany salvation. There are things that saved people do; and one of them is paying your tithe.

Some people say that all you have to do is give something from your salary, because God says He loves a cheerful giver. But in *2 Corinthians 9:7*, the apostle was not talking about tithe, because that was an acceptable thing in the church. He was talking about our attitude in giving our tithe. He was saying we should give it joyfully and willfully, counting it a privilege to give to the work of God.

Why Should We Pay Tithe?

Well, as you have observed, it is because the Scripture says we should do it. We are obligated by the Word of God to pay tithe. Those who are true children of God must obey the Bible. We give to care for the servant of God, whose work is to minister unto us the Word of God. We read in **Nehemiah 13: 10-12**, *"And I perceived that the portions of the Levites and the singers that did the work, were fled everyone to his field. Then contended I with the rulers and said, why is the house of God forsaken? And I gathered them together and set them in their place. Then brought all Judah the tithe of the corn and the new wine and the oil unto the treasuries."* We have a situation where the people of God stopped paying their tithe; therefore, those who ministered in the house of God had to leave and do secular work to maintain their families. So there was spiritual deterioration among the people of God because those who were supposed to do the work were not being taken care of. Therefore, the people did not have the pure Word of God; so they were living in a backslidden condition.

Once people stop paying their tithe, it is a sign that they are deteriorating spiritually; and they are not concerned with or about the work of God. Nehemiah says, "I contended with the rulers and said; why is the house of God forsaken?" My dearly beloved, we should never forsake the house of God, by not giving what we have been asked to give to God. Nehemiah said after he had contended with them, "then brought all Judah the tithe of the corn, the new wine and the oil unto the treasuries". I would like to remind you that it was only when they had everything in order in the house of God that they had true restoration and peace.

In *1 Corinthians 9: 4 -14,* the apostle Paul says; *"Have we not power to eat and to drink? Have we not power to lead about a sister, a wife, as well as other apostles, and as the brethren of the Lord, and Cephas? Or I only and Barnabas, have we not power to forbear working? Who goeth to warfare anytime at his own charges? Who planteth a vineyard, and eateth not of the fruit thereof? Or who feedeth a flock, and drinketh not of the milk of the flock? Say I these things as a man? Or saith not the Law the same also? For it is written in the Law of Moses, thou shall not muzzle the mouth of the ox that treadeth out the corn. Doth God take care for oxen? Or saith he it is altogether good for our sakes? For our sakes, no doubt this is written, that he that ploweth should plow in hope; and that he that thresheth in hope should be partaker of his hope. If we have sown unto you spiritual things, is it a great thing if we shall reap your carnal things? If others be partakers of this power over you, are not we rather? Nevertheless we have not used this power: but suffer all things, lest we should hinder the gospel of Christ. Do ye not know that they, which do minister about holy things, live of the things of the temple? And they, which wait at the altar, are partakers with the altar? Even so hath the Lord ordained that they which preach the gospel, should live of the gospel".*

This portion of Scripture cannot be clearer. The minister ought to be fed by the church. Paul used all manner of illustrations in this text to say the same thing: that the man who preaches the gospel must live by the gospel. I don't think I have to do much explaining of this text, unless I am addressing babes on this subject; maybe even they would understand this simple logic. But let us use another Scripture to clear any doubts that might be in our minds. *1Timothy 5:17 - 21* says, *"Let the elders that rule well be counted worthy of double honor, especially they who labor in the word and in doctrine. For the Scripture saith, thou shalt not muzzle the ox that treadeth out the corn, and the labourer is worthy of his reward. Against an elder receive not an accusation, but before two or three witnesses. Them that sin rebuke before all that others also may fear. I charge thee before God, and the Lord Jesus Christ, and the elect angels, that thou observe these things without preferring one before another, doing nothing by partiality"*.

Here again, the Scripture says that the minister of the Word of God should be properly taken care of by the church. It says they that labour in the Word and in doctrine should be counted worthy of double honor. Many commentators believe that "worthy of double honor" means double pay for the good work God's Ministers are involved in. The Scripture also discusses the discipline of the elder, and verse 21 says that we should "observe these things without preferring one before another, doing nothing by partiality". In other words, we cannot choose the portion of Scripture we like and leave out the portion that says we must take care of the servants of God.

We must pay our tithe so that the work of the Lord will not suffer. I am convinced that if the members of the church of the living God were paying their tithe, and the leadership was managing it well, there would be no lack in the House of God. But because we are being unfaithful to God in our tithes and offerings, the church cannot move forward as it should. In addition, a lot of pastors and leaders in the church have used other questionable methods of raising funds for the church. In my opinion, if the church were obedient to God in the area of tithe and offering, it would not have been necessary to use other methods to accomplish our goals in the church.

There are a lots of things to be done in the church. These include: taking care of utility bills, purchasing musical equipment - which by the way is very expensive and easily to damaged, building new churches, having crusades and feeding the needy; just to mention a few. The church of Jesus Christ can change its community by giving, togetherness, holiness and love for others. With our monies, we can meet lots of physical needs in our community. But, we must do it as the Bible says. Let us show the world the power of the church of the Living God, which is the Body of Christ on earth.

Giving Apart From Tithing

The Word of God says that we can rob Him not only in tithes, but also in offerings. Tithe does not belong to us. It is God's money, which we have been ordered to bring to His house. We cannot afford to take what belongs to the Lord and use it for our enjoyment. It does not belong to us. The offering that we give in the house of the Lord is our money; what we give to the poor and needy is our money. When God was ready to build the tabernacle, He told Moses to ask the children of Israel to bring an offering and He said specifically what kind of offering should be given. It had to be a freewill offering, from what belonged to them.

We read in **Exodus 25: 2 - 8**, "*Speak unto the children of Israel, that they bring me an offering: of every man that giveth it willingly with his heart ye shall take my offering. And this is the offering which ye shall take of them; gold and silver, and brass, and blue, and purple, and scarlet and fine linen, and goats hair, and ram's skins dyed red, and badger's skins, and shittim wood, oil for the light, spices for anointing oil, and for sweet incense, onyx stones, and stones to be set in the ephod, and in the breastplate. And let them make me a sanctuary; that I may dwell among them*".

So, this offering was left for them to decide what amount they should give; just as it is supposed to be today in freewill offerings. The giver decides the amount, but in tithing, God has already stated what He should get. And let us remember what **2 Timothy 3:16** says; "*All Scripture is given by inspiration of God, and is profitable for doctrine, for reproof, for correction, for instruction in righteousness*". So, there are countless Scriptures given for our instruction on tithing as well as on offerings. We cannot say the Bible is not clear on this topic. The Scripture is abundantly clear on the area of giving and tithing which are two separate things.

To build the tabernacle, the children of Israel gave in abundance. Moses had to ask them to hold back. These people saw their giving as a privilege and a way of saying thanks to God for delivering them out of bondage. They realized what they had, was given to them by God. They could have still been in bondage, but thank God they were liberated both physically and spiritually. Now, they did not say "We will need our money later in life". Remember, they were going to the Promised Land, and could have said, "When we reach there we will need to build something for ourselves and families".

Nor did they say, "well, we are in a desert, we need to build our own tents. We need extend our tents because our children are growing older and so we must put something aside for them". No! They gave willingly and with a heart of thanksgiving.

They did not doubt whether God had spoken to Moses or not. They did not question the need for the sanctuary. They just gave. Can I tell you something? When the Spirit of God is among the people of God, the people will feel the tug of God's Spirit in their lives, leading them to do the things that are right. I believe the people were stirred up by the Spirit of God to give. Moses, the man of God, was not afraid to tell the people what God had shared with him concerning the building of the tabernacle. Likewise, the pastor should not be afraid to tell the congregation what God says concerning giving in His House.

One of the problems in the church is our refusal to financially support the work of God. Yes, the Israelites built a tabernacle according to God's pattern, because the people gave, as God wanted them to. Some of us believe that if God wants His church built, He will provide the money to build it. Well, He wants His people to provide the money. God's people must build God's house, because the devil's people will build the devil's kingdom. Whether you are serving the true God, the Creator of heaven and earth and all that is therein, or the false gods made by man's hand (which is really the worship of Satan), they both require sacrifice.

Giving is part of our worship and it shows our devotion to our God. God is a giving God. He has given us all that pertains to life and godliness. He gave us His only begotten Son and the Scripture says in **Romans 8: 32**, *"He that speared not his own Son, but delivered him up for us all, how shall he not with him also freely give us all things?"* God has promised to provide all that we need. He is our source; therefore, we cannot be stingy with Him.

In the book of Exodus we read a strange story about the children of Israel in what we may call a backslidden state. Moses was on the mountain talking to God, but the Israelites said, "We don't know what has happened to him; so let us make gods that will go before us." *Exodus 32: 1 - 4* says, *"And when the people saw that Moses delayed to come down out of the mount, the people gathered themselves together unto Aaron and said unto him, up, make us gods which shall go before us, for as for this Moses, the man that brought us up out of the land of Egypt, we wot not what is become of him. And Aaron said unto them, break off the golden earrings, which are in the ears of your wives, of your sons and of your daughters, and bring them unto me. And all the people broke off their golden earrings, which were in their ears, and brought them unto Aaron; and he received them at their hand, and fashioned it with a graven tool, after he had made it a molten calf: and they said, these be thy gods O Israel, which brought thee up out of the land of Egypt"*. Isn't this unbelievable!

These people who were living in a backslidden condition, took the gold they were wearing, and willingly took them to Aaron to make a golden calf. If any pastor today were to ask his congregation to bring their gold and silver, to build a new sanctuary, he would be taking a big risk; and only God would be able to help him. First of all, many members of that congregation will say this is not of God; maybe even his assistant. The pastor will have a very difficult time convincing his congregation to donate their gold. The pastor may even run the risk of losing many members over that matter. Those wives who give will run the risk of losing their husbands; and most likely the story will become Headline News on the front page of every major newspaper, for weeks if not years to come.

But, here we read that Aaron told the people to bring their gold so that he could make them a god, and they brought their gold to him joyfully. Nobody had any problems with their actions except Moses, Joshua and God. The Bible says all the people broke off their golden earrings and brought them to Aaron. Everybody participated in this ungodly act happily. There were no quarrels, no murmurings and no Counsel meetings. Husbands, wives and children all participated. You see friends, the devil will influence people to support his cause and they will do it willingly. People will spend willingly on things that are ungodly, but when they come to the church of the living God they have all kinds of reservation.

This giving we read of here in *Exodus 32* was to build a false god. It was contrary to Scripture, but the backsliding people gave to it. God was annoyed to see that His people had turned away from Him and had given their money to advance the cause of the devil instead of His cause. What are you doing with "your" money? Are you helping to build the Kingdom of God while you are on earth and have life? Don't leave your money for another to use it for you. They may use it on false gods. God expects us to be faithful stewards. We have been given God's possessions to manage. We cannot waste what God has given to us because one day we will be called on to give an account of our actions here on earth.

Here is a story of a rich man who had a steward, who was unfaithful to his master's goods. This is what we read in **Luke 16: 1-12**; *"And he said also unto his disciples, there was a certain rich man, which had a steward; and the same was accused unto him that he had wasted his goods. And he called and said unto him; how is it that I hear this of thee? Give an account of thy stewardship; for thou mayest be no longer steward. Then the steward said within himself, what shall I do? For my lord taketh away from me the stewardship: I cannot dig; to beg I am ashamed. I am resolved what to do, that when I am put out of the stewardship, they may receive me into their houses. So he called every one of his lord's debtors unto him and he said unto the first; how much owest thou unto my lord? And he said, an hundred measures of oil. And he said unto him; take thy bill, and sit down quickly, and write fifty.*

Then said he to another, and how much owest thou? And he said, an hundred measures of wheat. And he said unto him, take thy bill and write fourscore. And the lord commended the unjust steward, because he had done wisely: for the children of this world are in their generation wiser than the children of light. And I say unto you, make to yourselves friends of the mammon of unrighteousness; that, when ye fail, they may receive you into everlasting habitations; he that is faithful in that which is least, is faithful also in much. And he that is unjust in the least, is unjust also in much. If therefore, ye have not been faithful in the unrighteous mammon, who will commit to your trust the true riches? And if ye have not been faithful in that which is another man's, who shall give you that which is your own?"

All men are God's stewards. Everything we have has been given to us by God - we only have them for a time. The things that have been given to us are earthly things, corruptible things, temporal things. They are not going to last forever. God is watching to see how we are managing the things that He has given to us. Because we are God's stewards, we will be asked to give an account of our stewardship here on earth. In the text, the steward was more concerned about doing his own will than that of his master's. We are more concerned about earthly things, than heavenly things. The steward was unfaithful in his lord's money. The church has been unfaithful in the area of money also. There always seems to be a reason why we cannot pay our tithes. But, if we are unfaithful in giving our tithes, I am not surprised that we are unfaithful in other areas of our lives also.

Some may say, "The salary is so small, that I cannot pay my tithe". You pay ten percent of that small salary. What does the Word say? "He that is faithful in that which is little, is also faithful in that which is much. And he that is unfaithful in little will also be unfaithful in much". If the salary is too small for you to give from now, when it is bigger, you will never give. It is not about big or small, rather it is a condition of the heart – you are either faithful or unfaithful. Now if you have a small store, and every day your clerk takes a little money from you, what would you do with that clerk? Would you remove that clerk from that small store, and take him to the place where you have more money? He is being unfaithful. Would you promote him? Of course not!

That is what some people are doing to God in His church. They are short changing God. They always have an excuse, and they say God understands, as if God approves their actions. God has set a standard and we must rise to it, God will not lower His standard for us. Some people are inconsistent – they give one month, and they don't give the next month. They are inconsistent. The Bible calls it unfaithful. Why do people take what belong to God, and use it for themselves? In that same chapter, we read about the rich man and Lazarus. The rich man died and went to hell – not because he was rich, but because his heart was not right with God here on earth. He left a lot of money behind, but that money could not redeem his soul. He misused his money on earth.

The pleasures of this world are for a short time: our houses will not last forever, and the parties will not last forever since the things of this world are temporal. Today you may have a job, and tomorrow the job may belong to someone else. We are stewards of what we have now, and we must give to God His portion. God will reward faithfulness but unfaithfulness will be punished.

Our riches on earth are not true riches. God is just using our riches to see whether or not we will be faithful to Him with them. Our true riches are in the other life - where no one can enter in or steal. It does not change hands there. I believe however, that there will be many persons who will never receive their true riches, because they are unfaithful with God's riches. The child of God cannot be part of both worlds - you cannot serve God and mammon.

When we "are friends" with worldly riches here, they will be able to help us here but not in the world to come. Money can be terrible when you love it more than God: when you love it so much that you take yours, and what belongs to God also. It is God who gave us power to get wealth. Why? He gave it to establish His covenant upon the earth; and for us to do His work. It takes money to accomplish God's purpose upon the earth, and God wants us to do our best in our life- time because it is only in this life that we can support God's work.

In **Matthew 17: 24 - 27** we read, *"And when they were come to Capernaum, they that received tribute money, came to Peter and said, doth not your master pay tribute? He said, yes. And when he was come into the house, Jesus prevented him saying, what thinkest thou, Simon? Of whom do the kings of the earth take custom or tribute? Of their own children, or strangers? Peter saith unto him, of strangers. Jesus saith unto him, then are the children free. Notwithstanding, lest we should offend them, go thou to the sea, and cast an hook, and take up the fish that first cometh up: and when thou hast opened his mouth, thou shalt find a piece of money. That take, and give unto them for me and thee"*.

In the Bible "a piece of money", refers to a large sum of money. Jesus says to Peter, pay your tax and mine from this money. Each time Jesus told Peter where to fish and he obeyed, he caught fishes in abundance. God wants to see obedience and faith in us – when there is faith and obedience, He will bless us. Money is not the problem. What we need is obedience and faith. Don't worry. God will provide. He knows where the money is or which raven to send to you with flesh in its mouth. This story about Peter is not ordinary. When we obey God, we will be blessed financially and otherwise.

The monies most people get monthly cannot make them millionaires. They need other doors to be opened. Obey God in your giving, and you will see supernatural miracles. We need to get God involved in our finances. Just as we need faith to be saved, so we need to sow in faith.

You must believe in God and He will bless the seed you sow. The farmer waits on God to send rain on the seed he sows. Lack of faith closes the windows of heaven but faith opens them. We must believe God in every area of our lives.

The Presence Of God & The Church

It is essential that we have the presence of God in the house of God. If we don't have the presence of God in the church, then it is not truly the church of the living God since it is the presence of God that makes it the House of God. Our flesh or our brilliance should not lead us - we need the Spirit of God to lead us. A church without the presence of God is a dead church; and God is not the God of the dead. Many are going through forms and rituals in the House of God, and are getting away with gross sins. Sin in our lives or in the church hinders or chases away the presence of God.

In *1Samuel 2: 12 - 26* we read; " *Now the sons of Eli were sons of Belial, they knew not the Lord. And the priests' custom with the people was, that, when any man offered sacrifice, the priest's servants came, while the flesh was in seething, with a flesh hook of three teeth in his hand: and he struck it into the pan, or kettle, or caldron, or pot; all that the flesh hook brought up, the priest took for himself. So they did in Shiloh unto all the Israelites that came hither. Also before* they burnt the fat, the priest's servants came, and said to the man that sacrificed, give flesh to roast for the priest; for he will not have sodden flesh of thee, but raw. And if any man said unto him, let them not fail to burn the fat presently, and then take as much as thy soul desireth; then he would answer him, nay, but thou shalt give it me now and if not, I will take it by force.

Wherefore the sin of the young men was very great before the Lord, for men abhorred the offering of the Lord. But Samuel ministered before the Lord being a child, girded with a linen ephod. Moreover his mother made him a little coat, and brought it to him from year to year, when she came up with her husband to offer the yearly sacrifice. And Eli blessed Elkanah and his wife, and said, the Lord give thee seed of this woman, for the loan which is lent to the Lord. And they went into their own home. And the Lord visited Hannah, so that she conceived; and bare three sons and two daughters. And the child Samuel grew before the Lord. Now Eli was very old, and heard all that his sons did unto all Israel; and how they lay with the women that assembled at the door of the tabernacle of the congregation. And he said unto them, why do ye such things? For I hear of your evil dealings by all this people. Nay, my sons, for it is no good report that I hear; ye make the Lord's people to transgress. If one man sin against another, the judge shall judge him: but if a man sin against the Lord, who shall entreat for him? Notwithstanding they hearkened not unto the voice of their father, because the Lord would slay them. And the child Samuel grew on, and was in favour both with the Lord; and also with men".

What a story about the sons of Eli. They esteemed themselves before the Lord and took for themselves before they gave to the Lord. They did not honor the Lord, rather they chose the best part for themselves. If the people did not give to them first, they took it by force. The Scripture says, "The sins of the young men were very great before God". When we put ourselves before God, it is a very great sin.

If you don't put God first, you would be like the sons of Eli, who, by their life style, caused the presence of God to depart from the temple of God. If you are not putting God first, you are a child of "Belial" – you don't know the Lord, and your sin is a great sin whether you be a member of the church or the pastor. You may feel it is not a great thing if you don't give God what He has prescribed in His Word, but the Word says it is a great sin. Why were their sins very great? For men <u>abhorred</u> the offering of the Lord. People abhor things that stink. They turn their eyes and noses away from it. It is like a dead, rotten carcass of an animal in the bushes. They avoid passing by it. Men abhorred the offering of the Lord and paid no regard to it. They were saying "This is not for me to observe". It is as if they were saying stop talking about putting God first – we must be first.

To abhor also means to reject; to cast out, to remove it from their midst; not thinking about it. In this case, they were rejecting a particular biblical principle, which teaches that God deserves the best and must be first. In essence, they were saying we don't accept this particular teaching. You may speak until "thy kingdom come", I will not accept it. You know, there are people like that up to this day in the church; who refuse to obey what the Scripture says. They want to have their own way in the church of the Living God.

While the sons of Eli were doing wrong in the House of God, there was a young child being raised to do the things that pleased God. The Scripture says, "But Samuel ministered before the Lord being a child". In the House of God, we must receive His Word as children. We must not resist the Word but rather, receive it with meekness. Children must take their place in the church of the living God, and minister to the Lord like Samuel. Begin to pray, sing, fast and be involved in the church like Daniel, Joseph, and so many others we have as examples. Jesus was twelve years old when He said, "I must be about my Father's business". He stayed in the church when his parents went home. The things of God occupied first place in His life.

While the sons of Eli were behaving badly, Samuel's mother made him a little coat. Here was a little child dressed up like a man of God - he grew in the House of God. The Scripture says that Eli heard all that his sons did; he spoke unto them but took no further action. He never disciplined them although they lay with the women at the door of the tabernacle. If there is no discipline in the church, then surely there will not be the presence of God in our lives because indiscipline chases away God's presence.

Without discipline, "Ichabod" will be written over the church - "the glory is departed". We all have to give an account to God, about how we dispensed our responsibilities in the church. We must not do things that will cause the people of God to transgress.

When we live in sin like the sons of Eli, we are putting barriers to the Spirit of God. We are making it difficult for the presence of God to be among us because sin repels the presence of God, and we are also causing others to stumble. In addition, we are giving the enemy occasion to blaspheme the name of our God. Without the presence of God, we cannot experience victory in the church of the living God.

It was Moses who said to God; "If your presence goes not with us, carry us not further". Because he knew the only way they could have been successful and victorious, was if the presence of God was with them. David besieged God. He said, "Cast me not away from thy presence; and take not thy Holy Spirit from me". The presence of God is essential for the church's success; and we must cherish His presence. Guard it with holy living, prayer and obedience to God's Word and Spirit.

The church without the presence of God is like a body without the human spirit. If it does not experience a miracle, it will decay. Unfortunately, many persons are decaying rapidly today and many ask why. But despite the reason, the Spirit of God has left and there is death. We must be conscious of the fact that the presence of God is among His people, therefore, we must conduct ourselves properly in the House of God. If His presence is with us, we must respect it. God always dwells in the Holy of Holies. There must be a hunger for God in our lives. Holiness, prayer, and a love for His Word must mark that hunger. When God sees that hunger, He comes and dwells in our midst.

My friends, I would like to remind you of what the apostle Paul says in *1Corinthians 1: 29*, "*That no flesh should glory in his presence*". In the presence of God, there must be humility. My dear brothers and sisters, we must approach God in humility. There cannot be holiness without humility – self must be laid at the altar of sacrifice. We must esteem others better than ourselves. We read in **Philippians 2: 4 - 8**; "*Look not every man on his own things, but every man also on the things of others. Let this mind be in you, which was also in Christ Jesus: who, being in the form of God, thought it not robbery to be equal with God; but made himself of no reputation, and took upon him the form of a servant, and was made in the likeness of men. And being found in fashion as a man, he humbled himself, and became obedient unto death; even the death of the cross*".

Before God, we are nothing. Let us not enter the presence of God like that Pharisee in **Luke 18**, who came in trying to justify himself before God. The Scripture says he went away empty. The "I am better than this brother" attitude of the Pharisee is found in the minds of many people who come to the House of God. We degrade others in order to pull them down, and to lift ourselves up.

We see from the Pharisee, that people could be in church praying, and their hearts are not right with God and man. Therefore, their prayers would not be answered. The publican, the Scripture says, fell on his face. He recognized that he was in the presence of God. He begged that his sins be forgiven him. Yes, he went home justified; he went home forgiven.

The Church & Worship

Maybe a good place to start our discussion under this heading is **Psalm 100**; *"Make a joyful noise unto the Lord, all ye lands. Serve the Lord with gladness: come before his presence with singing. Know ye that the Lord he is God: it is he that hath made us and not we ourselves; we are his people and the sheep of his pasture. Enter into his gates with thanksgiving, and into his courts with praise. Be thankful unto him and bless his name. For the Lord is good; his mercy is everlasting; and his truth endureth to all generations"*.

The heart of the child of God must be filled with gratitude. We must come to the House of God with thanksgiving. Jesus asked about the ten lepers who were healed, since all should have returned to give thanks, but only one of the ten returned to say thanks. We must not be ungrateful to God – thanksgiving is a must for the child of God. We must enter "His gates with thanksgiving". Each time we return to the House of God, we must remember among other things, to give him thanks. The Scripture says in **1Thessalonias 5: 16 - 18**; *"Rejoice evermore;*

91

Dr. Thomas Eristhee

pray without ceasing. In everything give thanks, for this is the will of God in Christ concerning you". In difficult circumstances, we still have to give God thanks. We must give thanks in the midst of disaster because God doeth all things well. When we give thanks, it causes us to put faith in God who can deliver us from all our troubles.

Thanksgiving is part of the Fruit of the Spirit. We have been called upon to enter "His gates with thanksgiving". The first stage of approaching God is giving thanks. Thanksgiving helps us to focus on God who has the answers rather than on the problem. However, The devil would like us to focus on the problem and be discouraged, but thanksgiving helps us to see the God who is able. Paul says, "In everything, by prayer and supplication with thanksgiving, let your requests be made known". Not only must we give Him thanks, but we must also give Him praise. To praise is to exalt the person of God: His attributes - who He is. We cannot have a relationship with God, without praising Him.

There are times in the book of Psalms, that the psalmist expressed lamentation, because he did not praise the true and living God. Praise is an act of glorifying or exalting God. It means to speak highly of Him. Praise is something vocal - you are lifting up God with your voice. Many Christians are afraid to lift up their voices and praise God, but this should not be so since the whole earth should praise God. To praise is to make a boast of. All our boasting should be of God. It involves the raising and the clapping of the hands and singing of praises to God. Shouting unto the Lord, David said in **Psalm 34:2**; "*My soul shall make her boast in the Lord: the humble shall hear* *thereof and be glad"*. We must acknowledge God in public and praise Him in the congregation of His people that they too would rejoice in the Lord, their God.

What a privilege we have to worship God. Man, I believe, is made up of three parts – body, soul and spirit. The tabernacle in the Old Testament had three courts or three dimensions: the outer court, the inner court, and the holy of holies. We enter the gates with thanksgiving, the courts with praise, and the most holy place with worship. We are talking about adoring, esteeming, magnifying, reverencing and bowing down before God. Everybody on earth worships something. For some, it is money for others it is false gods; for man's nature is to worship. But God demands that we worship Him and Him alone.

Worship is so important, that the devil is willing to give everything, or anything in return for it. That should tell us something about the importance of worship among the people of God. In the book of **Matthew 4: 8 - 10**, the Word of God says; *"Again, the devil taketh him up an exceeding high mountain, and sheweth him all the kingdoms of the world, and the glory of them; and saith unto him, all these things will I give thee, if thou wilt fall down and worship me. Then saith Jesus unto him; get thee hence, Satan: for it is written, Thou shalt worship the Lord thy God, and him only shalt thou serve"*.

The devil wanted worship; he wanted Jesus to worship him. He promised to give Jesus all the kingdoms of the world if He would only worship him. We are not getting into the theological argument of the text as to whether or not Satan had at that time the kingdoms of the world in his power or not. The point is, he is willing to give anything if he can get worship in return for it. Jesus himself made a very strong statement in this portion of Scripture about worship. He said, "Get thee hence, Satan: For it is written, thou shall worship the Lord thy God, and him only shall thou serve". Who or what we worship is who or what we will serve. The more we worship something or someone, the more our commitment to it increases.

Our worship proves our devotion to the things of God. When we worship things, we are literally worshipping the devil. Jesus said we must only worship God. Can you imagine hearing a statement like this from the Savior? In **John 4:23** Jesus says, *"But the hour cometh, and now is, when the true worshippers shall worship the Father in spirit and in truth: for the Father seeketh such to worship him"*. This portion of Scripture states, that God Almighty is looking for true worshippers. This is something He expects to get from His people. He is waiting for it.

Man's body relates to the world around him - the body is really for this world. Jesus had to take on a physical body to function here. To me, this is the outer court. Everybody sees the external - the outer court. Some say that the soul is man's self- conscious - the inner court. But, to the believer, God has made the spirit alive at the time of conversion. And we are supposed to communicate with Him through our spirit: "They must worship the Father in spirit and in truth".

God is Spirit, and our spirit must connect with God's Spirit. In true worship, we are connected to God. When we enter in true worship, there is a connection to the fountain that flows from the throne of God and out of our bellies shall flow "rivers of living water".

We see from the Old Testament that many of the people who were worshiping their false gods, sacrificed their own children, just to be accepted by these false gods –demons. For the church of Jesus Christ, worship is not just a tradition or a way that we have mastered, or an art that we have learnt. It is not a church culture. It is walking in the presence of the Holy God, and responding in the appropriate manner. I want you to remember that the true worshipper will worship God anywhere. But do not forget that when we come to church He expects us to respond properly in His presence. There is always a place that God has sanctified for His people to come into His presence collectively.

When we come before God, we must be clean. We must ensure that He has cleansed us. We have His righteousness. So we must come before Him with clean hands and pure hearts. Today, some people enter the church of the living God, just as if they are entering a theater; but, the building which the people of God dedicate to the worship of God, is not a theater. It is a very sacred place – the most sacred place on earth! When we come into the House of God, we do not come to meet with friends; rather, we come to meet with God; we do not come to view, rather we should come to participate. We must remember that we are in the presence of the Almighty God – God's domain – and not in a Courtroom.

Friends, it is your choice to worship or not to worship, but the Bible commands us to worship and serve the Living God. Even though you may not like to worship, you should go against your feelings and obey the Word of God.

Why Do We Go To Church On Sunday?

There has been a lot of propaganda about why Christians worship on the first day of the week. As a matter of fact, some people have even gone so far as to say that those who worship on Sunday are worshipping the Sun god. They have made the day that God Almighty has created as an "evil" day – they call it a day to worship Satan. I know my God did not create any day for the worship of Satan; and as far as I am concerned, we should be worshipping God every day of the week. But, we should never forget that the first day of the week plays a very important part in the life of the church of the Living God, regardless of what anybody else teaches. The Bible has spoken on this matter. So I want to give the reasons Christians go to church on Sunday.

One of the reasons is the fact that the resurrection of our Savior took place on a Sunday. We read in *John 20: 16 - 19*; *"Jesus said unto her, Mary. She turned herself, and saith unto him, Rabboni, which is to say Master. Jesus saith unto her, Touch me not; for I am not yet ascended to my Father. But go to my brethren, and say unto them; I ascend unto my Father, and your Father; and to my God and your God. Mary Magdalene came and told the disciples that she had seen the Lord, and that he had spoken these things unto her. Then the same day at evening, being the first day of the week, when the doors were shut where the disciples were assembled for fear of the Jews, came Jesus and stood in the midst, and saith unto them, Peace be unto you".*

We may debate the exact day that Jesus Christ was born, because the Bible is not specific about the exact day - so we can speculate. We can even debate the day He died. But when it comes to the resurrection, there should be no debate because the Bible is abundantly clear on that. The Bible states emphatically that it was "early, on the first day of the week". Let us read it from **Mark 16:9;** which reads, *"Now when Jesus was risen early the first day of the week, he appeared first to Mary Magdalene, out of whom he had cast seven devils".* I may not be sure about His exact age at the time of His death, but I do know that on the first day of the week, He rose from the grave; and I believe that the Holy Spirit recorded the day, because it is very important to us.

Why is a simple truth as this being ignored, and attacked by some who claim that they know the Scriptures? It hurts to know that people who should know better, refer to the day the Son of God arose from the grave, as the day the heathen worship the Sun god. We must go to the Holy Book "the Bible" and see what it says on the matter.

When Christ arose from the dead early on Sunday morning, He did not have to go to the emergency room at the hospital. He rose in victory! He rose triumphantly over death, the grave and the devil. He said to Mary, "Touch me not because I have not yet ascended to your Father and my Father", but later that same Sunday, He appeared unto the disciples; and that was after He had gone up to Heaven.

It was a Sunday that changed the lives of the dejected disciples. Joy came to them that Sunday when they saw the risen Lord. If Christ had not done all the miracles that He did, if He was not born of the Virgin Mary, and rose from the grave on Sunday morning, He would not have been God. The resurrection proved that He was God. Saturday reminded the Jews of their bondage, when God sent a deliverer by the name Moses to deliver them. Therefore, they were to observe a Sabbath in memory of that. My friends, the church of Jesus Christ gather on Sunday, not to remember Egypt, but to remember the resurrection of Jesus Christ.

Oh! How He suffered, bled and died at Calvary, for our sins. His enemies thought they had won the victory, that the church He said He would build would never happen, but Sunday morning brought victory! Jesus victoriously rose from the grave on Sunday morning, and that day was the greatest day ever for the church of God. That day changed the lives of the disciples. If there was no resurrection, there would be no church. So since the resurrection took place on Sunday morning, that day is very important for every child of God, and the world should rejoice because that day brought hope to the hopeless.

It was Sunday morning that changed their weeping into dancing. Jesus said unto Mary, "Why weepest thou?" Sunday is a day to celebrate the resurrection of the Risen Lord. This is not weeping time, but rather, a time to rejoice. The Lord is risen, He is risen indeed. It all happened on Sunday morning, early, on the first day of the week.

This is the greatest event of the church, and in history. I did not say of the Jews – I said the church, and in history. Paul talking about the importance of the resurrection said in **1Corinthians 15: 12 - 22**; *"Now if Christ be preached that he rose from the dead, how say some among you that there is no resurrection of the dead? But if there be no resurrection of the dead, then is Christ not risen: And if Christ be not risen, then is our preaching vain, and your faith is also vain. Yea, and we are found false witnesses of God; because we have testified of God that he raised up Christ: who he raised not up, if so be that the dead rise not. For if the dead rise not, then is not Christ raised: and if Christ be not raised, your faith is vain; ye are yet in your sins. Then they also that are fallen asleep in Christ are perished. If in this life only we have hope in Christ, we are of all men most miserable. But now is Christ risen from the dead, and become the first fruits of them that slept. For since by man came death, by man came also the resurrection of the dead. For as in Adam we all died, even so in Christ shall all be made alive".*

Paul says if Christ be not raised, everything we do as Christians is in vain. There is no hope without the resurrection of Christ; the resurrection is the heart of Christianity, and it took place on Sunday morning. My faith does not depend on keeping a Sabbath day holy. My faith is based on the fact that my Redeemer lives.

The tomb was empty on Easter Sunday. His disciples saw Him on Easter Sunday. They touched Him on Easter Sunday. The message on the first Easter Sunday was "we have seen the Lord. The Lord is risen, He is risen indeed". It all happened on Sunday. When believers die, we don't weep as those who have no hope. Because Christ rose from the dead, we too shall rise. The resurrection is the answer. There is nothing like the resurrection of Christ, to bring hope to the believers - dead and alive, and this important event took place on Sunday.

My dear friends, that was fulfilled in Jesus Christ. In *John 1:29* we read, *"The next day John seeth Jesus coming unto him, and saith, Behold the Lamb of God, which taketh away the sin of the world"*. When Christ died, He brought an end to all animal sacrifice; had He not risen, they would still be continuing in their sacrifices. The resurrection is the foundation of faith in Christ; there would be no true church if there were no resurrection. Remember He said, "I will build My church"; so the churches which were before the resurrection, were not His churches - and therefore, not true churches.

Secondly, the Holy Spirit was poured out on the church on a Sunday. The disciples asked Jesus Christ after His resurrection, whether He would restore the kingdom to Israel. Jesus responded in *Acts 1: 7 - 8*, *"And he said unto them, it is not for you to know the time or the seasons, which the Father hath put in his own power. But ye shall receive power, after that the Holy Ghost is come upon you; and ye shall be witnesses unto me both in Jerusalem, and in all Judea and in Samaria, and unto the uttermost parts of the earth"*.

This was fulfilled in Acts chapter two. From **Acts 2:1 - 6** we read; *"And when the day of Pentecost was fully come, they were all with one accord in one place. And suddenly, there came a sound from heaven as of a rushing mighty wind, and it filled all the house where they were sitting. And there appeared unto them cloven tongues like as a fire, and it sat upon each of them. And they were all filled with the Holy Ghost, and began to speak with other tongues, as the Spirit gave them utterance. And there were dwelling at Jerusalem, Jews, devout men, out of every nation under heaven. Now when this was noised abroad, the multitude came together, and were confounded, because that every man heard them speak in their own language"*.

It was fifty days after the resurrection of Christ that the Holy Spirit descended upon the disciples. Count fifty days after the Sabbath and you get Sunday. The two greatest events in the life of the church happened on Sunday - the descent of the Holy Spirit and the resurrection of Christ.

A lot of people are trying to put new wine into old bottles: Christianity into Judaism - but Christ says it cannot be done. We cannot put new wine into old bottles. Christ did not come to renovate the church; He did not come to add to the church. He said, "I will build MY church, and the gates of Hell shall not prevail against it". The church started with the death and resurrection of Christ and with the descending of the Holy Spirit. In *Acts 20:28* we read, *"Take heed therefore unto yourselves, and to all the flock, over the which the Holy Ghost hath made you overseers, to feed the church of God, which he hath purchased with his own blood"*.

Therefore, the church could not have been in existence before the death of Christ, because He purchased the church with His own blood. The church is not the Jewish religion. In *1Corinthians 12:13* we read, *"For by one spirit are we all baptized into one body, whether we be Jews or Gentiles, whether we be bond or free; and have been all made to drink into one spirit"*. The church is the body of Christ - believers from every nation, who put their faith in the Lord Jesus Christ, who have repented of their sins and have the Spirit of God living in them. You may think otherwise, but you cannot be saved if you don't have the Holy Spirit. It is not whether you observe a day - but rather, whether you have the Spirit. *Romans 8:9* says that it is not about a day. It is about the Spirit of God living in you every day. The same Spirit who descended on a Sunday when the disciples were in the upper room.

The Jews thought that their salvation was based on keeping a day holy. They thought this was their basis for standing right with God. But when the Holy Spirit descended on Sunday upon the disciples of Jesus Christ, all the religious people who came to the place and saw them were perplexed, because the Holy Ghost fell on the hundred and twenty followers of Christ, and not on the masses, which were at Jerusalem keeping the Sabbath day holy. He descended on Sunday and not on Saturday. On that very Sunday, three thousand of the Sabbath keepers got saved after Peter had preached unto them.

There was apostolic preaching on Sunday, which brought conversion - preaching under the anointing of the Spirit. These people who followed the Jews' tradition of worship, abandoned it, got saved and continued with the apostles. They did not go

103

back to their dead tradition. Therefore, we can say that the first church service took place on a Sunday. The first church sermon was preached on a Sunday. The first harvest of souls by the church took place on a Sunday. The first church baptism took place on a Sunday.

The Bible says in **Acts 2:41 - 42**; *"Then they that gladly received the word were baptized, and the same day there were added unto them about three thousand souls. And they continued steadfastly in the apostles' doctrine and fellowship, and in breaking of bread, and in prayers."* Friends, the reason that we worship on Sunday is obvious; however, what we need in every church of the living God is the Pentecostal fire that the apostles and the early disciples of Jesus Christ had. This will cause people to abandon their dead traditions and come to the church to gain life in the Spirit. When we come together, we do not come to remember Egypt - No! We come to remember Jesus Christ, His death and resurrection - that He arose for our justification and we rejoice in Him!

Paul kept the Sabbath before he got saved; yet, he was one of the biggest murderers in history. In **Galatians 4: 9 - 11**, he gives his view about the Sabbath and Jewish tradition after he got saved: *"But now after that ye have known God, or rather are known of God, how turn ye again to the weak and beggarly elements; whereunto ye desire again to be in bondage? Ye observe days, and months, and times, and years; I am afraid of you, lest I have bestowed upon you labour in vain"*. He called them weak and beggarly elements. He said that they brought people into bondage - not true liberty. He also declared that he was afraid for those who observed special days such as the

Sabbath; lest he had in vain bestowed labour upon them. He was saying in short that Judaism and Christianity cannot mix.

Thirdly, the early church worshipped on Sunday. *Acts 20: 6 - 8* reads, *"And we sailed away from Phillipi after the days of unleavened bread, and came unto them to Troas in five days; where we abode seven days. And upon the first day of the week, when the disciples came together to break bread, Paul preached unto them, ready to depart on the morrow; and continued his speech until midnight. And there were many lights in the upper chamber, where they were gathered together"*. We observe in this portion of Scripture that Paul spent a Sabbath with the believers. The Scripture says that they abode seven days there; but there is no record that they went to church on the Sabbath day or gathered together. But it is stated plainly that upon the first day of the week, when the disciples came together to break bread, Paul preached unto them; and continued his speech until midnight.

Some people are of the opinion that the believers came together to have a farewell party for Paul; but this is not what the Bible says. The Bible says that they came together to break bread - they came to have communion on a Sunday. Paul preached to them that Sunday. He was not a worshipper of the sun god but an apostle to the gentiles and he preached on a Sunday. We can see from this text that they broke bread, preached and even raised the dead on Sunday. In *1Corinthians 16: 1 - 2* we read, *"Now concerning the collection for the saints, as I have given order to the churches of Galatia, even so do ye. Upon the first day of the week let every one of you lay by him in store as God hath prospered him, that there be no gatherings when I come".*

Paul said, "I have given order to the "churches" of Galatia, even so do ye the same in Corinth." It was not one church that collected offering on Sundays - all the churches in that region collected offering on Sunday although Galatia was about 1000 km away from the city of Corinth. Today, Galatia is believed to be Turkey, while Corinth is in Greece. **1 Corinthians** was written about **60 A.D.** - less than thirty (30) years after the death of Christ. Yet, it was established that Sunday was a day of worship. In *Acts 2:7 - 11* the hundred and twenty that were filled on Sunday proclaimed the wonderful words of God that same Sunday and in *Acts 2:41*, those who accepted Christ on Sunday, after Peter preached unto them, got baptized on that same day.

Let us look at the conclusion of the whole matter by reading from the Holy Scriptures. *Acts 15:1 - 11* reads, "*And certain men which came down from Judea taught the brethren, and said, except ye be circumcised after the manner of Moses, ye cannot be saved. When therefore Paul and Barnabas had no small dissension and disputation with them, they determined that Paul and Barnabas, and certain other of them, should go up to Jerusalem unto the apostles and elders about this question. And being brought on their way by the church, they passed through Phenice and Samaria declaring the conversion of the gentiles: and they caused great joy unto all the brethren. And when they were come to Jerusalem, they were received of the church; and of the apostles and elders, and they declared all things that God had done with them.*

But there rose up certain of the sect of the Pharisees which believed saying, that it was needful to circumcise them, and to command them to keep the Law of Moses. And the apostles and elders came together for to consider of this matter. And when there had been much disputing, Peter rose up and said unto them, men and brethren, ye know how that a good while ago God made choice among us, that the Gentiles by my mouth should hear the word of the gospel, and believe. And God, which knoweth the hearts, bare them witness, giving them the Holy Ghost, even as he did unto us. And put no difference between us and them, purifying their hearts by faith. Now therefore, why tempt ye God, to put a yoke upon the neck of the disciples, which neither our fathers nor we were able to bear?" But we believe that through the grace of the Lord Jesus Christ, we shall be saved even as they".

Here, the sect of the believers who got saved from the Pharisees' movement wanted the believers to be circumcised and to keep the Law of Moses. Paul and his company said no. Thus, Sunday is not about Creation but about the New Birth. It is about the birth of the church. It is about Christ becoming the First Fruit. It was on Sunday that Jesus said to his disciples, "receive ye the Holy Ghost" (*John 20: 19 - 22*). It was also on Sunday that He commissioned His disciples to go and preach the Word (*John 20:21*).

In *Galatians 3: 1 - 7*, Paul writing to those who wanted to turn to legalism said; *"O foolish Galatians, who hath bewitched you, that ye should not obey the truth, before whose eyes Jesus Christ hath been evidently set forth, crucified among you? This only would I learn of you, receive ye the Spirit by the works of the Law, or by the hearing of faith? Are ye so foolish having began in the Spirit, are ye now made perfect by the flesh? Have ye suffered so many things in vain? If it be yet in vain; he therefore that ministereth to you the Spirit, and worketh miracles among you, doeth he it by the works of Law, or by the hearing of faith? Even as Abraham believed God, and it was counted to him for righteousness. Know ye therefore, that they which are of faith, the same are the children of Abraham".*

We started by faith, and we must continue by faith. When we stop living by faith, we will stop growing. The church will grow only if the church operates by faith. Some people will want us to operate in legalism and Judaism; and by so doing, hinder the work of the Holy Spirit in the church. This is not in the Scriptures. We see Jesus going to the Synagogue on a Saturday after His resurrection. Stand fast in the liberty Christ hath made you - you are free! Be not entangled again with the yoke of bondage.

Church Unity

Unity builds up; the more united the church is, the more effective it will be. In the Body of Christ, there should be no division. Therefore, the church should unite, because it is the Body of Christ. In the human body, every part functions for the good of the body. Similarly, in the church of Jesus Christ, every one must do their part for the glory of God. In **Psalm 133: 1- 3** the Scripture says, *"Behold, how good and how pleasant it is for brethren to dwell together in unity. It is like the precious ointment upon the head, that ran down upon the beard, even Aaron's beard: that went down to the skirts of his garments; as the dew of Hermon, and as the dew that descended upon the mountains of Zion. For there the Lord commanded the blessing, even life for evermore"*.

The Scripture says it is good for the brethren to dwell together in unity. But not just good, it says it is "pleasant". Yes! Because the church is the Body of Christ, there must be unity. The believers are the Family of God, because the same blood of Christ has washed every one, so there must be brotherly love.

The apostle Paul asked a serious question in *1Corinthians 1:13*; he says, *"Is Christ divided? Was Paul crucified for you? Or were ye baptized in the name of Paul?"* The obvious answer is: No! If Christ is not divided then His followers also should not be divided. Let us look at some Scriptures on the subject that will help us to see the importance of unity.

In *Leviticus 26:8* it reads, *"And five of you shall chase an hundred, and an hundred of you shall put ten thousand to flight: and your enemies shall fall before you by the sword"*.

Matthew 18:19 - 20 says, *"Again I say unto you, that if two of you shall agree on earth as touching anything that they shall ask, it shall be done for them of my Father which is in heaven. For where two or three are gathered together in my name, there am I in the midst of them"*.

Whenever the people of God unite, there is victory. It is like the dew of Mount Hermon: the dew keeps the mountain fresh and fertile causing it to be fruitful. So, unity keeps the children of God fresh and fruitful. For the Lord bestows His blessings. When the church unites, God will pour out His blessings upon it.

The principle of having unity to succeed is all around us. It is a universal principle. When the church unites, it is very strong - nothing can stop it. In the book of Genesis, we have a great lesson on unity. Maybe, the greatest lesson in the entire Bible on unity.

Let us read the verses found in *Genesis 11:1-9*. *"And the whole earth was of one language; and of one speech. And it came to pass, as they journeyed from the east, that they found a plain in the land of Shinor; and they dwelt there. And they said one to another, Go to, let us make a brick, and burn them thoroughly. And they had brick for stone, and slime had they for mortar. And they said, Go to, let us build us a city and a tower, whose top may reach unto heaven; and let us make us a name, lest we be scattered abroad upon the face of the whole earth. And the Lord came down to see the city and the tower, which the children of men builded.*

And the Lord said, Behold, the people is one, and they have all one language; and this they begin to do: and now nothing will be restrained from them, which they have   imagined to do. Go to, let us go down, and there confound their language; that they may not understand one another's speech. So the Lord scattered them abroad from thence upon the face of all the earth, and they left off to build the city. Therefore is the name of it called Babel; because the Lord did there confound the language of all the earth: and from thence did the Lord scatter them abroad upon the face of all the earth".

This was after the flood had destroyed man from the face of the earth. Noah and his sons obeyed the command of the Lord to be fruitful and replenish the earth. But here in chapter 11, these men rebelled against the commands of the Lord, and decided to settle in one particular place, than to scatter over the face of the earth. They decided to build for themselves a city and a tower. They wanted the tower to reach heaven; it was a very ambitious project. So, to put it in proper perspective, the unity that they had was to do something ungodly, against the commands of the Lord. Yet, they would have achieved their goal, if God had not come down and put division among them.

Why were they going to achieve this unbelievable goal? Because there was unity – they had one language. My dear friends, there cannot be unity if there is no understanding. We must try to understand each other. If we are going to have unity, there must be proper communication between all concerned. Now the Bible demands that the children of God should endeavor to keep the unity of the Spirit in the bonds of peace. The church must do all in its power to keep the unity of the Spirit. Why were they building the tower? Some people believe that they were building it in anticipation of another flood – that if it ever rained like it did, they would survive.

In addition, there are others who believe that it was a communication center, where they would communicate with the gods. They wanted to be close to the gods – the sun, moon, and stars. It is believed that Nimrod was foremost in the building of Babel, Babylon – a religious system that led to the worshipping of false gods that rebelled against the God of heaven and earth. Abraham was also involved in idol worship, but God called him out from among them.

It is written in *2 Corinthians 6:17-18*, *"Wherefore, come out from among them, and be ye separate saith the Lord, and touch not the unclean thing; and I will receive you. And will be a Father unto you, and ye shall be my sons and daughters, saith the Lord Almighty"*.

In other words, in order for God to receive us, we cannot stay in a system which rebels against God. We cannot stay in a religion where the blind leads the blind – We must be born again. Why are you saying this, you ask? There is a spirit among some churches today, where there is no discipline and any thing goes; yet they expect the people of God to unite with them, because they call themselves "the church". But, this is not the kind of unity God wants His church to participate in. As a matter of fact, this kind of unity will destroy the church of the living God. We must remember that oil and water do not mix – light and darkness cannot agree. There is a common belief that doctrine does not matter. But, my dear friends, must we seek to keep the unity of religion? No! We must seek to keep the unity of the Spirit, the unity of common faith!

The unity of Babel was self- centered. Their unity was not for the furtherance of the Kingdom of God; it was for their glorification. Their plan was pride. They wanted to build a house that had a foundation on earth, where the top reached heaven, and they all agreed to do it. They wanted a name for themselves, they wanted to be men of renown – so they were united to do wrong. It would seem that we always know how to unite when we want to do things for ourselves; but the things of God always lag behind. It is always the faithful few who will come out to do the things of God. This ought not to be so.

They did not know the Scripture found in *Psalms 127: 1* *"Except the Lord build the house, they labour in vain that build it: except the Lord keep the city; the watchman waketh but in vain"*. Yes, confusion was the end of the place they started building. They spent much time and resources, but in the end they never completed it because the Lord confused them. What is that thing that you are building that God does not approve of? The text says the Lord came down to see what they were building; it does not say that He did not know what they were building.

What will God find us building when He comes down? Now, He already knows what we are building. Some of us are building our own kingdom and we don't want to associate with any body else. Pastor, founder, builder and owner – we are all. We have nobody to give account to and many of us do things that displease the Lord. But, He will come down one day and we will have to give an account of our actions, therefore, let us all do the things that will make us acceptable in His sight. We need unity in our midst. We cannot do without it even though we may feel we do not need any other church or organization to exist.

When the people of God unite, they succeed. When unbelievers unite, they succeed also. Even the devil knows the power of unity, and uses it to his advantage. Friends, the principle is universal. This is what Jesus says about unity when the Pharisees accused him of casting out devils by Beelzebub. *Matthew 12: 25 - 30* reads, *"And Jesus knew their thoughts, and said unto them; every kingdom divided against itself is brought to desolation; and every city or house divided against itself shall not stand: And if Satan cast out Satan, he is divided against himself; how shall then his kingdom stand? And if I by Beelzebub cast out devils, by whom do your children cast them out? Therefore they shall be your judges. But if I cast out devils by the Spirit of God, then the kingdom of God is come unto you; or else how can one enter into a strong man's house and spoil his goods, except he first bind the strong man? And then he will spoil his house. He that is not with me is against me; and he that gathereth not with me scattereth abroad".*

Here Jesus shows that Satan will never cast out Satan. In the kingdom of Satan, they are united to do evil; never good – and Satan is never on God's side. But the portion I really want us to concentrate on is from **verses 43 – 45** of that same passage which read, *"When the unclean spirit is gone out of a man, he walketh through dry places, seeking rest, and findeth none. Then he saith, I will return into my house from whence I came out, and when he is come, he findeth it empty, swept and garnished. Then goeth he, and taketh with himself seven other spirits more wicked than himself, and they enter in and dwell there and the last state of that man is worse than the first. Even so shall it be also unto this wicked generation".*

The devil knows the power of unity, and uses it for his benefit. Here, we read that when a demon is cast out from an individual, it goes about seeking a resting place – somewhere else – but if he does not succeed, he comes back to the house from which he was cast out. If he finds it vacant (meaning the Lord is not there and there is an opening for the demon to return), he goes out to get seven other demons more wicked than him, to help him occupy this house and defend it victoriously. Because he has more demons with him, the fight is greater since he now has more confidence because he has a "team" with him. What a lesson for us as a church to learn that even the demons unite to get their job done. Thus, we too should unite to advance the Kingdom of God.

In the Kingdom of God, every member of His church must pull his weight; and should never cause division in the church of the living God. In the book of **Romans 16: 17 - 18** the apostle Paul says, *"Now I beseech you brethren, mark them which cause divisions and offences contrary to the doctrine which ye have learned, and avoid them. For they that are such serve not our Lord Jesus Christ, but their own belly; and by good words and fair speeches deceive the hearts of the simple"*. Here Paul says that we must mark those who cause division in the Body of Christ. And the word "mark" seems to suggest to paint with a color that you can see afar off so that you cannot miss them (a neon color). Also, it says that we must avoid them; don't be part of them; do not mingle with such individuals. The Scripture sees them as trouble - makers.

1 Corinthians 1:10-13 says, *"Now I beseech you brethren, by the name of our Lord Jesus Christ, that ye all speak the same thing, and that there be no divisions among you: but that ye be perfectly joined together in the same mind and in the same judgment. For it hath been declared unto me of you, my brethren, by them that are of the house of Chloe, that there are contentions among you. Now this I say, that every one of you saith, I am of Paul, and I of Apollos; and I of Cephas, and I of Christ. Is Christ divided? Was Paul crucified for you? Or were ye baptized in the name of Paul?"* He said, I charge you, I implore you, I call upon you; and he did not call upon them in his own name, but in the name of the Lord Jesus Christ - that they all speak the same thing, and that there be no divisions among them. That they be perfectly joined together in the same mind and judgment.

As a church, we must have that same mind and we must follow the divine social program. In this portion of Scripture, the division was about the different ministers the church had known over the years, and who had baptized whom. My dear friends, we are all laborers in the Kingdom of God; we should not seek disciples after our own selves. The cross of Jesus Christ does not divide – it unites His people. In Christianity, we all look to the cross and that is what brought blessing to us all. When there is division among the people of God, it makes the cross of Christ of none effect. One of the greatest evils in the world today, is to make the cross of Christ of no effect. When brothers and sisters cannot unite, it gives the idea that the cross of Christ has no power.

Jesus said, "If I am lifted up, I will draw all men unto Me". The Spirit of the cross is not one of division; it is not of self-ambition and pride. It is one of humility, self-sacrifice and unity. Division is opposed to the true spirit of Baptism. Were you baptized by Paul's name? No! You were baptized in the name of the Father, Son and Holy Spirit. Division comes when there is carnality among us, when our relationship with God is not up to-date. According to *Ezekiel 37*, bones must come together. All must find their place in the Body of Christ. When that is done, we will have a mighty revival in the church and in the nation.

Unity is something we must all work to achieve in our personal lives, and in the church of God. We will marvel at what God will do in His church if we are able to achieve this unity. Therefore, we should pray for unity in His church. The church of Jesus Christ is alive, and I believe in these last days we need to put the proper machinery in place in the church; and when this is done we will see the glory of God in His church.

Dr. Thomas Eristhee

Let unity flow like the crystal river, let it flow like that oil that ran from Aaron's beard; let it flow between husband and wife; children and parents, among young and old. Let nothing hinder the flow of the Spirit of God in the church of the living God.

Conclusion

Friends, it hurts my heart to see the church not meeting the needs of the day, because we are not functioning the way Christ wants His church to function. The problem is not with Christ, nor with the Bible but with us. We need to get back to the Bible to see the way the early church functioned and was administered. This is what we have to follow. Modernism, secularism, worldly wisdom and lack of spirituality are killing the church of God.

We are not experiencing what God wants us to experience in the church. God has revealed what His church should be like, so that we could play our part in His church as He has ordained; and that we will not walk in darkness as it relates to the church. You shall know the truth and the truth shall set you free! So, I say to you: Let us turn back to God and His Word with all our hearts, and He will abundantly pardon us.

About the Author

The life of Thomas Eristhee from the time of his conversion has been a mystery to many. This was a young man who had no desire for the things of God and who thought most of the church folks were hypocrites. However, from the time he got serious with God, his life has been growing.

He is now the Bishop of the Pentecostal Assemblies in his nation. He travels extensively throughout the Caribbean, South America, Canada, U.S.A. and Africa, preaching the gospel and ministering in Conferences. He holds a Diploma from the West Indies School of Theology, and a Graduate Diploma of Ministry with Glory Word Seminar in Malaysia. He received his Bachelor of Arts Degree from the Caribbean College of the Bible International. He also attended the Stephen Olford Center for Biblical Preaching, U.S.A. He received his Master of Ministry Degree with Trinity Theological Seminary, U.S.A, and his Doctor of Ministry with Covington Theological Seminary, U.S.A.

Dr. Eristhee is a man who greatly fears God and believes in righteousness and true holiness. He is a humble servant of

God. He and his wife Midran, are happily married and have one daughter - Shimea. They are involved in the work of the Lord together

www.ingramcontent.com/pod-product-compliance
Lightning Source LLC
Chambersburg PA
CBHW020252290526
45784CB00003B/1221